FERNÁN CABALLERO

by Lawrence H. Klibbe

Cecilia Böhl de Faber, more popularly known by her pseudonym of Fernán Caballero, is the creator of the modern Spanish novel and the first important novelist who successfully directed this genre from Romanticism toward Realism after 1850. She also emerges in this study as the first feminist of modern Spanish literature and as an equal of her contemporaries, George Sand and George Eliot. Her literary friendship with Washington Irving during the latter's residence in Spain (1828-1829) provided encouragement and stimulus for some important early writings. This period before the publication of *La Gaviota* (1849) and *La familia de Alvareda* (1856), her two major novels, shows that Fernán Caballero had prepared many compositions long before their appearance in magazines and as books. Her father, a famous German Hispanist living in Spain, and her Spanish mother, a bold advocate of women's rights, also encouraged the young writer. Fernán Caballero's personal life, tragic and somewhat obscure primarily because of the deaths of three husbands, is nonetheless revealing about this unusual woman's inner strength and artistic persistence. She dominated popularly and critically the Spanish novel during the otherwise barren period from 1850 until 1870 when Realism will begin to triumph, thanks in large part to the literary career of this woman with the masculine pen name, Fernán Caballero.

ES

(TWAS 259)

TWAYNE'S WORLD AUTHORS SERIES (TWAS)

The purpose of TWAS is to survey the major writers —novelists, dramatists, historians, poets, philosophers, and critics—of the nations of the world. Among the national literatures covered are those of Australia, Canada, China, Eastern Europe, France, Germany, Greece, India, Italy, Japan, Latin America, the Netherlands, New Zealand, Poland, Russia, Scandinavia, Spain, and the African nations, as well as Hebrew, Yiddish, and Latin Classical literatures. This survey is complemented by Twayne's United States Authors Series and English Authors Series.

The intent of each volume in these series is to present a critical-analytical study of the works of the writer; to include biographical and historical material that may be necessary for understanding, appreciation, and critical appraisal of the writer and to present all material in clear, concise English—but not to vitiate the scholarly content of the work by doing so.

ABOUT THE AUTHOR

Lawrence H. Klibbe received his Ph.D. from Syracuse University and is currently on the Romance Languages faculty of New York University. He has published *James Russell Lowell's Residence in Spain, 1877-1880,* and has coedited an edition of Gustavo Adolfo Bécquer's *Rimas y leyendas.* He has written for various journals, such as *Hispania, The Modern Language Journal,* and *Thought,* and reviews books regularly in *Books Abroad.* He also works for the New York City Board of Education as an examiner in foreign languages.

Fernán Caballero

By LAWRENCE H. KLIBBE

New York University

Twayne Publishers, Inc.   ::   New York

To Gerard and Dotti

Preface

Cecilia Böhl de Faber, more popularly known by her pseudonym of Fernán Caballero, is generally acknowledged as the creator of the modern Spanish novel, or, at least, as the first important novelist during the nineteenth century who successfully directed the novel from Romanticism toward Realism. However, critics seem divided about the precise contributions of Fernán Caballero to the theory and practice of Spanish prose fiction, and critical questions have been raised about the positive and negative influences of her literary output. More accurately, perhaps, the problem emerges about the extent to which Doña Cecilia adhered to the familiar patterns of Romantic, traditional, and local color examples to the exclusion of European novelistic productions at this time, especially in France and England. The popularity and influence of Fernán Caballero's extensive writings helped to establish the direction of the Spanish novel, but these orientations could potentially, on the one hand, have been toward a richer, broader vision of this literary genre or, on the other hand, toward a less rewarding and less international future for the novel after 1850. The purpose of this book, then, is to present a survey of the role played by Fernán Caballero in the development of the Spanish novel during the nineteenth century.

The approach toward some conclusions about the above questions is primarily analytical subsequent to the first chapter. This chapter is devoted to the literary background, the exceptional parents, and the life of Cecilia Böhl de Faber with the aim of elucidating information and explanations about the writer's ideas, beliefs, and development. The two novels, *La Gaviota* (*The Sea Gull*) and *La familia de Alvareda* (*The Family of Alvareda*), which brought Fernán Caballero early popular success and favorable support from critics, receive each a chapter with detailed analysis and critical commentaries; they would seem to merit this careful treatment because they are still judged as her most significant contributions to Spanish literature. The other novels, since they are considered as integral parts of the complete artistic trajectory of Doña Cecilia, are summarized and studied in a following chapter. The shorter prose pieces are treated generally rather than individually for an understanding of this writer's interests, enthusiasm, and views within another single chapter. Finally, the concluding chapter provides a brief summation of the previous investigations, some observations about the woman and the writer, and the effort to trace the fortunes among critics of Fernán Caballero, particularly at the present time.

In the case of Fernán Caballero, several scholarly problems are immediately evident in addition to the critical issues about her contributions to the Spanish novel; and attention is given to the questions of the various editions of the works, the dates of composition and publication of the novels, the many letters available for a more comprehensive study of this unusual woman, and the reliability of some sources. However, this book is an endeavor to offer an overall view of Fernán Caballero rather than a painstaking attempt at new scholarship. Resolution of the above questions, problems, and issues must lie outside the scope of this book—by necessity and by choice. At the same time, the author's hope is that this book will provide some inspiration and a great deal of stimulus for any future students of this first feminist of modern Spanish literature.

It has been difficult occasionally to determine exactly how to classify Fernán Caballero's fiction, whether as novel or short story. She herself at times apparently could not decide. For her editors this poses the unhappy problem of determining typography, whether to italicize her works as novels or put titles between quotation marks as short stories. Our decision has been, perhaps wrongly at times, to maintain consistency by italicizing all the titles of her works.

All translations from the Spanish are my own throughout the text.

Finally, I must thank New York University for the sabbatical leave to see this project to completion and my colleagues for their cooperation during my absence, and also a word of appreciation to Professor Gerald Wade for his patience and gentle reminders.

LAWRENCE H. KLIBBE

New York University

Contents

Chronology

1796   December 25 or 27: Cecilia born at Morges, Switzerland.
1803   Johann Nikolaus Böhl von Faber, Cecilia's father, named Hanseatic consul to Cádiz.
1805   Family moves to Hamburg, Germany.
1806   Francisca de Larrea Böhl von Faber returns to Cádiz with two daughters. Cecilia and her brother remain in Hamburg with their father.
1810   Attends French boarding school administered by nuns in Hamburg.
1812   Mother returns to Germany.
1813   Family united permanently in Cádiz.
1816   Father named consul for Hamburg in Cádiz. Cecilia married to Captain Antonio Planels Bardají, an army officer; they are sent to Puerto Rico.
1817   Husband's death.
1818   Return to Cádiz. Trips to Germany and France.
1822   Marriage to Francisco Ruiz del Arco, Marqués de Arco-Hermoso, and residence in Sevilla and nearby Dos Hermanas.
1828   Introduction to Washington Irving during the latter's stay in Spain and the beginning of a literary friendship with the American author. A first draft in German of the novel *La familia de Alvareda* (*The Family of Alvareda*).
1834   Writing of essays and short stories, some included in later novels, indicated in correspondence, but earlier compositions of writings also evident.
1835   Second husband's death. *La madre o El combate de Trafalgar* (*The Mother or the Battle of Trafalgar*), a short story, probably translated by her mother, published in Spanish.
1836   Father's death. European travels in Portugal, France, Belgium, and England. A short, unhappy love affair in London with an English noble, identified by letters as "Federico Cuthbert."
1837   Marriage in Spain to Antonio Arrom de Ayala.
1838   Mother's death.
1840   The short story, *Sola* (*Alone*), published in German in Hamburg. Financial problems result in husband's business trip to the Philippine Islands and subsequent long separations of the couple.

1845   Writing of the novel *La Gaviota* (*The Sea Gull*).

1849   Publication of nine novels, stories, and an essay: *La Gaviota* (*The Sea Gull*), *Elia*, *Una en otra* (*One in Another*), *Peso de un poco de paja* (*Burden of a Little Straw*), *La hija del sol* (*The Daughter of the Sun*), *Los dos amigos* (*The Two Friends*), *La suegra del diablo* (*The Devil's Mother-in-Law*), *Una excursión a Waterloo* (*An Excursion to Waterloo*); and a first version of *La familia de Alvareda* (*The Family of Alvareda*) as *La familia Alvareda* (*The Alvareda Family*) in magazine form.

1850   Publication of further novels and stories: *Lágrimas*, *Callar en vida y perdonar en muerte* (*Silence in Life and Pardon in Death*), *El ex-voto* (*The Ex-Vow*), *No transige la conciencia* (*No Compromise with Conscience*), *El albañil* (*The Mason*), *El marinero* (*The Sailor*), and a pirated edition in New York of *La familia de Alvareda*.

1851   Publication of the stories *Con mal o con bien a los tuyos te ten* (*Stay with your Own in Good and Bad*), *Matrimonio bien avenido, la mujer junto al marido* (*In a Harmonious Marriage, the Wife Is at the Side of her Husband*), and an essay *El Eddistone* (*The Eddystone*).

1852   Publication of two novels, *Clemencia, Lucas García*, and customs sketches: *Cuadros de costumbres populares andaluces* (*Popular Andalusian Local Color Sketches*).

1853   Increasing money worries despite husband's appointment as consul in Sydney, Australia. Publication of two novels, *Simón Verde*, *Más largo es el tiempo que la fortuna* (*Time Is Longer than Fortune*), and a corrected edition of *Lágrimas*.

1855   Publication of *La Estrella de Vandalia* (*The Star of Vandalia*), *Un verano en Bornos* (*A Summer in Bornos*), *Justa y Rufina* (*Justa and Rufina*), *Las dos gracias* (*The Two Graces*), and *Tres almas de Dios* (*Three Souls of God*), the first title for the later *Un servilón y un liberalito* (*A Loyalist and a Liberal*), all novels.

1856   Publication of *La familia de Alvareda* for the first time in book form with a prologue by the Duque de Rivas.

1857   Residence in the Alcázar of Sevilla provided by Queen Isabel II in recognition and friendship. Publication of stories *Lady Virginia*, *Relaciones* (*Relations*), another *Cuadros de costumbres* (*Local Color Sketches*), and the beginning of active collaboration in the review, *La Educación Pintoresca* (*The Picturesque Education*).

1858   Husband's return to Spain. The completion of *Obras completas*

(*Complete Works*), Mellado, Madrid, 19 volumes, that had been started in 1855.

1859   Husband's suicide in London because of many business and financial reverses. Publication of a definitive edition of *Un servilón y un liberalito*, and the *Colección de cuentos y poesías populares andaluces* (*Collection of Popular Andalusian Short Stories and Poems*).

1861-   A new edition of *Obras completas* in 16 volumes by the same
1864   publisher, Mellado.

1863   Publication of the novel, *La farisea* (*The Woman of the Pharisees*). Noticeable increase in translations (English, French, and German) of various works by this date.

1865   A new edition of *La farisea* brings the largest number of sales of any previous book, and the novel *Las dos gracias* reaches four editions. *Obras completas* in 14 volumes begun, not to be completed until 1893, by a new publisher, Sáenz de Jubera, Madrid.

1868   Revolution of 1868 and abdication of Isabel II cause loss of residence given by the Queen, and economic circumstances cause difficulties in the declining years.

1877   April 7: Death at Sevilla.

CHAPTER 1

The Woman and the Writer

IN the case of Fernán Caballero, a discussion of the literary background during the first half of the nineteenth century is very necessary because the intellectual heritage provided by her father, active in the Romantic Movement, is likewise associated closely with the various developments of Spanish literature during this period. A mother, also committed to the issues of the time, an international education, and choice of homes gave Cecilia Böhl de Faber an exceptional, fortunate, and profitable childhood and youth.

I The Young Cecilia

Some conflicting evidence places in doubt the exact day of Cecilia's birth at Morges, Switzerland, in 1796; it was either December 25 or 27 during her parents' trip to Germany from Spain after their marriage in the early spring of that year.[1] Cecilia Francisca Josefa was not baptized until March 13, 1797 at the parish church of St. Jean d'Echallens in the diocese of Lausanne, a date considerably later than usual after a child's birth, because of the absence of a Catholic church near Morges. The family left Switzerland at the end of the winter, spent a short time in Hamburg, Germany, and returned to Spain by the autumn of 1797, setting up a home in Chiclana near Cádiz in Andalucía.

Three more children, Aurora (1800), Juan Jacobo (1801), and Angela (1803), were born during this residence in southern Spain. These years were apparently very happy and tranquil ones for the young Cecilia, and no major problems disturbed her childhood despite the social and political turmoil in Europe and necessarily in Spain. Johann Nikolaus Böhl von Faber, after his brother's death from yellow fever in 1800, took full charge of Comercial Böhl, the family business in Cádiz, a firm going back to the middle of the eighteenth century. Cádiz enjoyed a

13

central location as a leading cultural as well as commercial city for Spain during these years.

A large family, business difficulties because of the Napoleonic wars, and an inclination toward literature rather than commerce caused Böhl von Faber increasing worries. Some relief came in 1803 when he was named Hanseatic consul in Cádiz, and this post as an official representative of the loose confederation of some German states gave Böhl von Faber status, influence, and some financial gain. Shortly thereafter, and for reasons that are not entirely clear, he purchased property in Görslow near Hamburg, and in 1805 the entire family moved to that city. The bleak political situation would seem to be a logical reason for this change of residence and Böhl von Faber's return to his homeland. In the same year, the battle of Trafalgar further enmeshed Spain in Napoleon's ventures, and the country was rapidly becoming a battleground.

The transfer to Germany did not suit Cecilia's mother, and the latter in 1806 returned to Cádiz with two of the children, Angela and Aurora. Again, the motives of this swift and radical move seem complex: temperamental and psychological differences existed between husband and wife; climate and national dissimilarities must have influenced the decision; and, perhaps of most importance, the matter of business considerations. Trade and travel were suffering as France and England intensified their wars, and Napoleon seemed at the peak of his power after Austerlitz. The separation of the couple was not intended to be long and was not meant to be definitive.[2]

The education of Cecilia began at this period to come under two influences after the previous experiences of maternal supervision in a Spanish setting—experiences which proved to be influential also for her future development. The influence of her father provided an inspiring source of learning and knowledge, not only about European culture but also about Spanish literature, for Böhl von Faber was initiating a career as a leading Hispanist and scholar. This example of a loving, encouraging father showed Cecilia the values of an international education, and she was later to recall on numerous occasions the decisive influence of Böhl von Faber on her intellectual formation. A further influence came through the formal education Cecilia received in Hamburg, where she was placed in a private school administered by nuns who had fled from France because of the Reign of Terror. The training was of course strict and religious, and Cecilia's later adherence to and defense of the Church must have found roots in the lessons of this boarding school.

Seven years, 1806-1812, almost to the day, passed before the Böhl von Fabers were reunited in Germany with the return of Cecilia's mother. This time the explanation for such a prolonged separation is logical and clear: the War of Independence, beginning with the popular insurrection in Madrid on May 2, 1808 against the French occupation, had prevented any travel from Cádiz to Hamburg; and the slow decline of Napoleonic power after the retreat from Moscow brought some improvement in normal communications between the various European countries. Cádiz was in fact converted into a stronghold of the liberal elements trying to hold together the country for the legitimate king, Fernando VII, and at the same time attempting to effect some democratic reforms in the future management of the nation. Böhl von Faber's business interests in Cádiz were a shambles after this period of warfare; and his financial enterprises in Germany were equally disastrous, so that by 1811 he had to sell the estate in Görslow to satisfy his creditors. The Napoleonic period, in short, resulted in the almost total financial ruin of Böhl von Faber; and only his wife's return at the end of 1812 lifted his spirits.[3]

In 1813 the entire family returned finally to Cádiz where Böhl von Faber liquidated the family business, took a position with the English firm of Duff Gordon, and moved to nearby Puerto de Santa María. Cecilia's formal education was now terminated, but the three years, 1813-1816, were marked by the excitement of observing the strange, exotic world of her childhood after the restrained atmosphere of Germany and a religious school. She became as ardent a convert to the Hispanic world as her father upon the return to Cádiz and Andalucía.

II *Johann Nikolaus Böhl von Faber*

The remarkable career of Böhl von Faber merits attention in all histories of modern Spanish literature, and his part in the emerging Romantic Movement, or at least the Romantic Revival, deserves consideration and recognition. Undoubtedly, the ideas of Böhl von Faber represent a significant aspect in his daughter's literary formation at this particular date during her childhood in Germany. By the time Böhl von Faber came back to Spain in 1813, he had decided to abandon business as his main interest in favor of literature and, more especially, Spanish literature as a source and reflection of the Romantic spirit.[4] It is perhaps no coincidence that, after a long emotional crisis, he became a convert to Catholicism in 1813, which obviously must have pleased his wife, children and friends, both business and social, in Spain. This year, then, marks a sharp change in Böhl von Faber's life—a change important for Spanish literature and his daughter's contribution to it.

Böhl von Faber, born in Hamburg in 1770, had received an excellent education from private tutors, a married couple named Campe, who were famous for their advanced pedagogical ideas, based largely on Rousseau and Locke. Showing extraordinary progress the young Böhl von Faber also began to study literature with particular enthusiasm. However, he was destined for the family firm at Cádiz and went there in 1785. He began to immerse himself in Spanish culture, especially the Classical literature of the medieval and Golden Age eras, which were downgraded by the ruling Neoclassical literary circles. His courtship of a lively Spanish girl, Francisca de Larrea, a native of Cádiz, began around 1790; but the marriage did not take place until early 1796. Böhl von Faber's views were at variance with the liberal expressions of his wife, and he complained on occasion about her advocacy of women's rights and an independent career beyond the confines of domestic duties.[5] These conflicts, apparently never overt, must have been somewhat obvious to Cecilia, especially after the definitive transfer to Cádiz in 1813, and the stimulating atmosphere with these attendant differences is certainly another important and unusual aspect of her background. Indeed, no study of Fernán Caballero can fail to take into serious account the fascinating, conflicting attitudes of the parents.[6]

The long separation of Böhl von Faber and Doña Frasquita encouraged him to continue his curiosity about Peninsular literature, and the Romantic stirrings, centered in large measure in Germany, coincided with his previous investigations. German

Romanticism, Spanish literature, and Catholicism seemed to merge in his mind toward a crisis, religious and psychological, which finally resulted in his conversion as a Catholic, a growing avocation as a German Hispanist, a dedicated Romantic, and the desire to reside permanently in Spain, where he could contribute to the cultural climate.[7] When he settled again in Andalucía in 1813, Böhl von Faber immediately and decisively entered the arena where Romanticism and Neoclassicism were slowly coming into conflict.

III *Francisca de Larrea*

Some critics have surmised that the marriage between Fernán Caballero's parents was not very happy, but the evidence for such a sweeping and difficult conclusion is really not available.[8] In any event, the intellectual and philosophical differences of her parents provided a brilliant setting for stimulating influences upon Cecilia, and it is reasonable to conclude that the parents, with their varying discussions and readings, must have exerted a strong, worthwhile force by reason of their broad, opposing arguments. However, the facts of domestic frictions are not eliminated as an element of the marital situation of the Böhl von Fabers; but whether these admitted differences were the normal confrontations of most married couples or more serious antagonisms is not clear. There appears to be no doubt that the husband and wife, going at times along divergent paths, became one of the most popular couples in the social and cultural life of Cádiz.

Doña Frasquita, born in 1775, was the daughter of a Spanish father and an Irish mother, and she had studied in England and France. This exceptional background of Cecilia's mother, who knew English and French well, could only influence for the better the daughter's cosmopolitan education and cultural interests. Doña Frasquita became very committed to the goals of women's rights, and her husband—indicating thereby a source of their marital differences—complained about her admiration for books on feminism, such as Mary Godwin's *Vindication of the Rights of Women,* an influential tract of the times from England.[9] The wife's residence in Cádiz without her husband from 1806 until 1812 gave her perhaps the chance, under the guise of patriotism and nationalism, to become very active in the defense of the city against the French. She kept up a correspondence with her absent husband, organized *tertulias* or social gatherings, and composed some interesting writings as indications of her intellectual liberation. The pieces reflect the relevant issues of Doña Frasquita's particular plight: *Una aldeana española a sus compatriotas* (*A Spanish Townswoman to her Compatriots*), *Saluda una andaluza a los vencedores de los vencedores de Austerlitz en los campos de Bailén* (*An Andalusian Woman Greets the Conquerors of the Conquerors of Austerlitz on the Fields of Bailén*), and *Andalucía, una visión* (*Andalusia, a Vision*). The elements of loyalty toward traditional Spanish characteristics and a tendency toward local color sketches of Andalucía—outstanding features of Fernán Caballero's literary work—are already seen in the mother's writings, which Cecilia logically must have read probably after 1813.

Although Doña Frasquita failed to keep pace with her husband's many literary activities after 1813, she continued to write compositions, reflecting again her daughter's future ideas, which are conveniently grouped as *Visiones* (*Visions*), *Diálogos* (*Dialogues*), *Sucesos y tipos dramáticos* (*Dramatic Events and Types*), and *Esbozos de tipos populares* (*Sketches of Popular Types*). Politics, literature, and nature were Doña Frasquita's principal themes. She vigorously opposed the revolutionary spirit, exemplified by Napoleon, who had invaded Spain and who had thereby destroyed or damaged the traditional roots of Spanish life, the absolute monarchy, the Church, and the conservative habits of the provinces, especially Andalucía. Again, the formative qualities of Fernán Caballero's art stand revealed in her mother's literary efforts after 1813, when the influence upon the young daughter could be felt at first hand despite the more striking success of Böhl von Faber as an advocate of Romanticism.[10]

IV *The Romantic Battle*

Neoclassicism's short-lived triumph in the eighteenth century, with its lack of popular appeal and failure to produce the requisite number of literary masterpieces, faced a new challenge in the second half of the century from the Romantic or, more precisely, Pre-Romantic stirrings in other European countries. In Spain, the Romantic characteristics represented basically many of the same themes and sentiments that had appeared in the literature of the Golden Age. The writers, poets for the most part, were still under the influence and direction of Neoclassical mentors; and their literary products are a blend of the two worlds of Neoclassicism and Romanticism. If the nineteenth century opens conveniently for historical and literary studies in 1808, the first third of the century is nevertheless characterized by no clear rupture with Neoclassicism. The faint stirrings of the Pre-Romantic spirit went no further than that because the disruptive and liberalizing political struggles from 1808 until 1814, followed ironically by the tyranny of Fernando VII until 1833, effectively prevented Romanticism from crossing the Pyrenees. On the other hand, the exile of young liberals and rebels by Fernando, labeled by his adherents *El deseado* ("The Desired One") brought them into contact with European Romanticism and when, upon the King's death, they returned to Spain in 1833, completely won over to Romantic ideals, Romanticism triumphed quickly and easily. Some critics, indeed, say that Spanish literature of the nineteenth century does not commence until 1833.[11]

The groundwork, however, had been prepared in these intervening years, 1808-1833, for Spanish imitations, influences, and original treatments of the European literary achievements. Romanticism was prepared for acceptance by several figures who labored to overcome the lingering but stubborn Neoclassical domination of Spanish cultural life. Their work consisted of international and historical investigations of the Romantic Movement: international by dint of European acceptance of Romantic ideals as a common meeting ground; and historical as a realization that Romanticism advocated ideas and themes already in Spanish literature from medieval and Golden Age sources. This appeal to the national and patriotic spirit, in fact, won advocates by urging rejection of the foreign, and more particularly the French, doctrines in favor of native or indigenous sources. The revival of the national past was certainly indicated by Tomás Antonio Sánchez who published *El poema del Cid* (*The Poem of the Cid*) in 1779 and later prepared other editions of medieval literature; by Bartolomé José Gallardo who brought Spanish bibliography to a scientific status, particularly by his many references to the richness of Old Spanish in the *Ensayo* (*Essay*), published posthumously, and still an invaluable source for investigations; and by Agustín Durán who compiled between 1828 and 1832 one of the notable collections of ballads, *Romancero general* or *Romancero de Durán* (*General Book of Balladry* or *Book of Balladry of Durán*). The journal, *El Europeo* (*The European*), 1823-1824, popularized the European Romantics, such as Scott, Schiller, and Byron, and also provided an outlet for the writings of young Romantics in Spain. The contribution of other newspapers and reviews and the increasing wealth of translations into Spanish of Scott, Hugo, and Cooper also stimulated the growth of the Romantic Movement. In 1830 the first historical novel written in Spain under the direct influence of Scott was published, *Los bandos de Castilla, o el Caballero del cisne* (*The Bands of Castile, or the Knight of the Swan*) by Ramón López Soler, a former editor of *El Europeo*. The importance of the *emigrados* or exiles from the rule of Fernando VII also resulted in a double influence in that the Romantic concept of Spain as an exotic, medieval land was conveyed to Europeans. London and Paris were the most popular places of residence for the refugees, so that it is no accident that a principal tenet of the returning Romantics after Fernando VII's death became Hugo's definition of Romanticism as Liberalism in literature.

These years, 1814-1835, which saw the growing strength of the Romantic Movement and the triumph, especially in the theater, of Romantic ideals coincided with Böhl von Faber's noteworthy additions to the new currents. His Romantic affinities in Germany first came to maturity with his favorable reputation as an astute book collector who was amassing one of the most valuable private libraries in Spain. Doña Frasquita's literary and social circles undoubtedly were made aware of her husband's acquisitions and the volumes already on hand. Böhl von Faber published *Floresta de rimas antiguas castellanas* (*Collection of Ancient Spanish Poems*) in 1821 with two additions in 1823 and 1825, forming thereby an anthology of one thousand poems with notes; and in 1832, *Teatro español anterior a Lope de Vega* (*Spanish Theater before Lope de Vega*), twenty plays of Juan del Encina, Gil Vicente, Bartolomé de Torres Naharro, and Lope de Rueda. These works, still valid sources of Spanish literature, would have sufficed to establish Böhl von Faber's place in the Romantic Revival.

However, Böhl von Faber had earlier joined battle against the

Neoclassical ideas in a more public and controversial display of opposing viewpoints—the *querella calderoniana* ("Calderonian Quarrel").[12] In 1814, he had published in a Cádiz review a translation of August Wilhelm von Schlegel's *Über dramatische Kunst und Literatur* (*On Dramatic Art and Literature*) as *Reflexiones de Schlegel sobre el teatro* (*Reflections of Schlegel on the Theater*), a critical manifesto of European Romanticism, promoting the merits of the Spanish Golden Age theater, in particular that of Lope de Vega and of Calderón. Schlegel classified the Spanish drama as "Romantic," comparable to the plays of Shakespeare, in poetry and thought; and the German especially praised Calderón as the apex of Spanish dramatic achievement. He further urged Spaniards to study their Golden Age for an understanding and inspiration of the Romantic heritage which had been ignored and downgraded by the Neoclassical advocates during the eighteenth century. José Joaquín de Mora, who ironically provided Fernán Caballero with his help in later life, attacked Böhl von Faber in a series of articles about the virtues of Calderón and Romanticism. The "quarrel" or polemics went on sporadically until 1818, when both foes attacked and counterattacked in different magazines. Antonio Alcalá Galiano, before his acceptance of Romanticism and staunch defense of Romantic theories, allied himself with Mora. No victor was announced when the Böhl-Mora controversy ended in 1819; but the Romantic ideas—ideas which were coming of age—could not be eliminated by the old literary order, and Böhl von Faber's arguments were considered superior. At any rate, Böhl von Faber's election in 1820 as an honorary member of the Real Academia Española (Royal Spanish Academy) seemed to afford a confirmation of his victory in this quarrel over the place of Calderón in Spanish literature and Spanish Romanticism. Happily, no personal animosities were permanently aroused between the polemicists; and Mora, somewhat like his ally Alcalá Galiano, altered his opinions in the following years to an eclectic approach or a middle path between Neoclassicism and Romanticism.

By 1820, Böhl von Faber's personal and financial life had also improved considerably in addition to the above-mentioned triumphs in the literary and cultural spheres. Doña Frasquita, apparently after a period of friction, had aided him greatly in his many enterprises, especially with Cecilia's nascent literary attempts. Cecilia's two sisters and brother married happily and also found well-to-do spouses. The remaining years of Böhl von Faber until his death in 1836 seemed successful and tranquil; and Doña Frasquita's death in 1838, while concluding the fascinating, influential, and stimulating lives of this couple, now signified that Cecilia could no longer look to her parents for their previous help, encouragement, and love in her personal and literary experiences.

V *Unlucky in Love*

Cecilia, during these years between 1813 and 1836-1838, surely became cognizant of the interesting roles of her father and mother in Spanish society and intellectual life. Apparently, she felt a closer bond with her father, perhaps because of the unfortunate separation of mother and daughter during the latter's childhood in Germany. However, there is no reliable biographical documentation about Cecilia's life and experiences from 1813 until 1816, although the logical conclusions are that she, like her parents, immersed herself completely and happily in the daily social activities of her environment. The period certainly provided a background of political and cultural ferment with the defeat of the French in Spain, the end of Napoleon's influence in Europe, the restoration of the Bourbon monarchy under Fernando VII, the return to a peacetime way of life, and, of course, the Romantic battle with her parents as active participants.

In 1816, Cecilia married Captain Antonio Planels Bardají, an army officer, from a rich family of Ibiza, who, at the age of 26, seemed to be an ideal husband for the increasingly prominent Böhl von Faber. In fact, Böhl von Faber in this same year was named consul for Hamburg in Cádiz, and his status, if not his immediate financial situation, rose in the esteem of Spanish society. Again, the evidence is lacking for any conclusive statements about this tragic marriage for Cecilia; and she, in later years and in a literary rendition, perhaps expressed at least this accuracy after the events: "I then, I can readily say it, was *good*, as one who came from a French boarding school established in Germany, and I could bring forth from my heart and from my experience the *debut* in life which I have given to the Clemencia of my novel."[13]

Her reference to the heroine of her novel, *Clemencia*, as well as the internal evidences of many resemblances between the book and the life of Fernán Caballero, have led critics to rely by necessity on this source. The role of her parents, the romantic glow of youth, and the dashing appeal of a military uniform led probably to the hasty marriage of Cecilia on March 30, 1816. Almost twenty years old, she was certainly at a very marriageable age at that time in Spain. Her husband was psychologically unsuited as a husband for a sensitive, cultured, idealistic girl like Cecilia, if *Clemencia* can be accepted as accurate authority. His immaturity, arrogance, insensitivity, and mental cruelties shocked and disillusioned the young bride; and the couple's transfer to Puerto Rico, where he was posted, must have been another traumatic experience for Cecilia, removed from the protective setting of home and parents.[14]

Fortunately for Cecilia, the adage of "Marry in haste, repent at leisure" did not condemn her long because her husband died of apoplexy in Puerto Rico on July 24, 1817. The young widow returned to Spain the following year, further shattered by her first direct contact with the death of someone close to her. Her somber mood was relieved by trips to Germany and France from September of 1819 until October of 1820, where she had the opportunity to revisit childhood scenes, renew old friendships, and broaden her interests by a variety of scenes and places, included on several occasions in her future writings. The return to Cádiz marked the courtship of Cecilia by Francisco Ruiz del Arco, Marqués de Arco-Hermoso, who had been possibly interested in her prior to the marriage of 1816 and who had certainly started to see her before the European trip. At any rate, Cecilia became the wife of the Marqués de Arco-Hermoso on March 26, 1822.

VI *Marquesa de Arco-Hermoso*

The years of Cecilia's marriage to the Marqués de Arco-Hermoso until his death on March 17, 1835 were the happiest times of her life from many points of view. Her parents, of course, were overjoyed at the prospects of this second marriage—

almost the opposite situation of the unpleasant union with Planels. Apart from the personal aspect of this second marriage, Cecilia took an important step up the social ladder, whether or not she gave primary consideration to this consequence of accepting the Marqués de Arco-Hermoso as her new husband. Although she described her spouse as an ideal mate, evidence is available that Cecilia did not feel for him *une grande passion* or think of him as "her one and only love," clichés which might characterize her latent romanticism or her psychological scars after the first marriage. She certainly portrayed him very favorably in *Clemencia*—a very different person than the unfortunate Planels—as the respectful and generous aristocrat who sincerely loved her.

These years brought Cecilia security, stability, the management of households, travel, and many opportunities to observe different ways of Spanish life. She entered the best salons of Sevilla, which found reflection in *La Gaviota* (*The Sea Gull*); and she enjoyed the country existence at nearby Dos Hermanas, which would provide her with the material for *La familia de Alvareda* (*The Family of Alvareda*). Cecilia, as a result of these changes of residence from the city to the country, observed constantly and astutely the many differences between these two Spains. This polarization of Spain into two camps, beginning as a convenient point of reference with the arrival of the Bourbons in 1700, was sharply dividing the nation, unable to cope with the deteriorating political situation and a resultant lag in material progress during a century of enormous strides among other European powers.

Ironically, then, the period of Cecilia's most felicitous times was the historical moment in which Spain was obviously sinking deeper in the quicksand of disaster. In these same years, the colonies in South America fought successfully for their independence, and by 1825 Spain had lost almost all the loyalties and wealth of the once-great empire. At home, the internal tension, resulting from that split in the previous century between the Europeanizers and the traditionalists, was starting to produce an era of inept governments (succeeding each other in quick rotation), mediocre monarchs, and civil wars that made impossible a united nation. Fernando VII, "the king desired by all," as his loyal subjects proclaimed him in defiance of Joseph

Bonaparte as King of Spain, proved an ungrateful ruler when he returned in 1814 as the legitimate successor of the Bourbons. Callously ignoring the sufferings and sacrifices of his exhausted people, Fernando VII embarked upon a reign of repression and authoritarianism in an attempt to restore the autocratic rule of the Bourbons of the eighteenth century. He abrogated the Constitution of 1812, accepted by all factions in Cádiz as a hope and compromise for a modern Spanish state, and in 1823 accepted a French invasion to restore him to power after a rebellion—an ironic twist to the events of 1808-1814. The last ten years of Fernando VII's reign until his death in 1833 witnessed harsh treatment for those at home and a sad exile abroad for opponents of this king, so wrongly called *el rey deseado de todos.*

By abrogating the traditional Salic law to permit the accession of his daughter, Isabel II, *El deseado* created a crisis more tragic and complicated for Spain because the forces of the young Queen and the partisans of Don Carlos, the king's brother, struggled sporadically but bitterly during the coming years for control of the country. Isabel II, in order to gain support for her cause, granted slowly and grudgingly concessions to the liberals and moderates who wanted change, reform, and the Europeanization of the nation. However, the generals, knowing their needed power to maintain the weak Queen on the throne, intervened repeatedly and increasingly without any success in the government. Spain careened from government to government, from prime minister to prime minister, and Isabel II devoted herself—probably in frustration and despair—to a life of luxury and unexemplary behavior.

What were the reactions of Cecilia, her husband, the Böhl von Fabers, and their social circles to these events in the national life? Cecilia's literary views were formed and influenced to a significant extent by the contemporary atmosphere, in addition to the influence of her parents and her education at school and abroad. Böhl von Faber, despite his enthusiastic Romanticism, was a foreigner in love with Spain, traditional and conservative —a mood adopted by Cecilia. Doña Frasquita had lived through the French invasion and occupation, especially noticeable in Cádiz, and adhered strictly to religion, monarchy, and tradition as the bases of national strength. Cecilia, willingly or not, must have been cognizant and appreciative of her parents' points of views; her training in a religious school and her impressive reactions (like her father's) to the strange, exotic world of southern Spain, particularly after their return in 1813, were molded in the pattern of a conservative traditionalist. As the Marquesa de Arco-Hermoso, Cecilia belonged to the social class with vested interests in the preservation of the old order. It is no wonder then that she followed the path of political and social conservatism as a writer—and thereby set the Spanish novel in a certain direction.

Her years, then, as the Marquesa de Arco-Hermoso are the central years for her initiation, development, and definitive formation as a writer.[15] She did not suddenly appear spontaneously as a writer in 1849, although of course this year marks the publication of a major novel, *La Gaviota*, and several other important and interesting literary endeavors. Montesinos[16] has very conclusively demolished this myth about Fernán Caballero's emergence as an author. At the same time, the background of Spanish literature, dominated during her second marriage by the triumphant Romantic Movement and the timid *costumbrismo*, is indeed explanatory about reasons and aspects of Fernán Caballero's art. The characteristics of both movements, one major and the other secondary, according to generally accepted criticism, demonstrated unquestionably to the young woman various devices in her fledgling literary endeavors during these years— and later.

Romanticism in Spain is conveniently granted the dates between 1833 and 1849—between the theatrical triumph of the Duque de Rivas and his fellow exiles and the publication of *La Gaviota*. This generalization, debatable and simplistic, can be interpreted nevertheless as a certain number of years (without the requirement of a precise year as a starting and ending point) during which Romanticism emerged victorious or at least dominant from the struggle with Neoclassicism. The movement, of course, lasted briefly as any semblance of a school or established mode of literature; but Romanticism, as a trait of literature, entered the mainstream of the modern Spanish novel after 1849 and lingered fitfully in the works of Galdós and other Realists. Of course, one may generalize by saying that Romanticism represents the "opposite" of Neoclassicism in the sense that the former aimed at a complete change from the past and that the Romantics deliberately accepted and utilized the ideas which the Neoclassical adherents abhorred. These literary characteristics of Romanticism, with individual variations among the Romantic artists, may be succinctly described as individualism or the emphasis upon the "I," the subjective; the imagination, unhampered necessarily by the believable, or the fantastic, mysterious, and supernatural; the Middle Ages as a favorite setting for plots, this period representing the exotic, unfamiliar, and strange; the hero doomed to tragedy, an antisocial or idealistic person; fate overwhelming man no matter how much he struggles through will, reason, or logic; nature in its picturesque, unique qualities with the more hostile elements, such as night and storms; a mixture of the ugly or grotesque with the beautiful or sublime; a belief in social, political, and moral progress; appeal to the emotions and the sentiments rather than the intellect, with the "heart" preferred to the "head" as a guide; and liberty or freedom for the rights of man in all spheres of his interests and activities. These features, of course, represent the Romantic Revolt in general—a different brand of Romanticism from the Romantic Revival urged by Böhl von Faber and personally familiar to the now Marquesa de Arco-Hermoso.

However, these elements in the exuberant outpourings of the early Romantics, even prior to 1833, were logically known to Doña Cecilia, in addition to her knowledge of the other European Romantic productions in the original versions or in translations. Closer to home than Romanticism, with its influences and coincidences in European sources, was the *costumbrismo,* slowly appearing in the newspapers and magazines. *Costumbrismo,* lacking an exact, equivalent term in English, may be defined as the fabrication of local color sketches, or as a realistic observation in prose of the life of the times—with all facets, physical and psychological, as theme material, for the objective or subjective reactions and conclusions of the *costumbrista,* the practitioner of the art. Thus, the writer of these sketches had certain liberties within the limited space allotted to the essayist in a journal; and the *costumbrista,* appealing to the new mass audience of newspaper readers, could earn money by judging accurately the tastes of the middle classes. The *costumbrista* sketches, then, are closely associated with the rise of newspapers and increas-

ingly popular material; they also represent journalism entering
seriously into the field of literature. Of course, *costumbrismo*
can be said to have had its origins earlier, in the eighteenth century; Addison and Steele's *Spectacular Papers* in England and
Washington Irving's *Sketch Book*, closer in chronology, might be
cited as evidence. *Costumbrismo* had really started to flourish in
the period before Fernando VII's death and Romanticism's
definite acceptance as a method to escape censorship, imprisonment, or exile because the authorities tended to tolerate the
short, guarded criticisms of contemporary conditions and life.
Later, *costumbrismo* developed into a more important treatment of society, habits, and people in the approximate period,
1833-1849. The *cuadro de costumbres* stressed description with
a predominant tone of local color and respect for Spanish traditions; the *artículo de costumbres* inserted a realistic critique of
problems and customs with an added note of satire. Both types,
whether a "picture" or an "article" about customs, offered a
realistic return to a principal characteristic of Spanish literature; and this realism was exploited by successful *costumbristas*,
such as Serafín Estébanez Calderón, Ramón de Mesonero Ro-
manos, and Mariano José de Larra, the master of this genre.

Doña Cecilia's thirteen years of marriage to Arco-Hermoso,
spanning these developments in contemporary literature, are
lacking in letters by her (only two apparently survive), in
surprising contrast to the heavy correspondence after 1849 so
that "the beginnings of Fernán Caballero as a writer are a vast,
penumbral zone" and "we only know with certainty essays,
written or rewritten, when the author was approaching forty,
but very little about the awakening of her literary curiosity."[17]
This awakening, if not earlier, occurred evidently a short time
after her second marriage in 1822 and undoubtedly before 1828.[18]
An earlier date than 1822 is of course possible but is lacking in
any precise evidence; the date of 1828 for the existence of some
writing exercises is accepted because of the documentation about
Washington Irving's meetings with Böhl von Faber and his
daughter, the Marquesa de Arco-Hermoso.

VII   *An American in Andalucía*

Washington Irving's first residence in Spain from February
11, 1826 to August 23, 1829 has been studied on several occasions,

and the importance of this period has been long recognized as a critical phase of his literary development.[19] Also, his use of Spanish sources, themes, and settings belongs not only to American literature, but to the brilliant era of nineteenth-century American Hispanism with George Ticknor and Henry Wadsworth Longfellow. However, from the point of view of Spanish literature, Irving's visit to Spain, studied and documented carefully, has interest and importance because he was accepted by the Böhl von Faber circles of scholars and writers.

This record is the most valuable observation of Fernán Caballero at the moment that she was initiating her literary career— her material as yet unpublished but in its formative stage. Ironically, Irving's primary curiosity centered on Böhl von Faber's activities, a logical curiosity in view of the latter's reputation as a Hispanist, and Irving's similar Romanticism. The rapport, excellent immediately, continued between the two men in Puerto de Santa María and other Andalusian places during the two years, 1828-1829; and the tantalizing question, of course, is the possible influence exerted by Böhl von Faber upon his American visitor. However, the primary consideration is the friendship between Irving and the Marquesa de Arco-Hermoso whom he met on December 30, 1828 and visited on the following day: "Call this morning... on the Marchioness of Arco-Hermoso, make a long visit, the Marchioness relates many village anecdotes of the village of Dos Hermanas. Return home & make a note of them."[20] The evidence that Irving jotted down notes for several of Fernán Caballero's stories, especially *La familia de Alvareda*, is very conclusive as a witness of her awareness and her utilization of the treasure of local color in Andalucía. Whether the *costumbrista* and narrative interests and sources of Fernán Caballero played an active role in Irving's own writings are moot questions, so far beyond any solid proof.

Irving's help to Fernán Caballero during their extensive conversations seems to have been limited primarily to encouragement, exchange of views, and a general affinity of outlook toward the employment of regional, popular, and national elements in literature—an affinity shared with Böhl von Faber. The American's impressions of the Spanish marchioness as expressed in a note to her father reveal his own astute psychology and also provide a vivid portrait of the woman at a turning point in her literary career:

It is with the greatest satisfaction that I have made the acquaintance of your daughter the Marchioness of Arco-Hermoso. I was extremely struck with her strong resemblance to you, not merely in her countenance, but in the strength and vivacity of her feelings, in her mode of expressing herself, and in the apparent turn of her mind. I propose to pay a visit to Dos Hermanas in the beginning of next week. The bad weather and the wretched state of the roads have hitherto prevented me. The Marchioness, I understand, has had the goodness to write out some little anecdotes she told me of the Spanish peasantry, their opinions and mode of life. She related them with wonderful spirits and discrimination, and *in fact* her conversation made such an impression on me that I noted down as much of the substance and point of it as I could recollect. I do not know when I have been more delighted with the conversation of any one, it was so full of *original matter*, the result of thinking, and feeling, as well as observing.[21]

It is of interest that, aside from any flattering comments about daughter to father, Irving (the words in italics are his own underscored remarks) had grasped quickly and correctly certain basic ideas of Fernán Caballero's works: observation, local color material, enthusiasm of feelings, and forceful expression. Continuing to be impressed by Doña Cecilia and showing that the previous reactions were not isolated instances, Irving later wrote that she had "warmth and purity of heart" and "an unworldly spirit, rarely met with in one who has mingled so much with the world. The Marchioness delights me continually, the freshness and vivacity of her feelings and the zeal with which she expresses them, on all subjects in which she takes a real interest." Also, in the same letter, the American guest realized the impact that the Böhl von Fabers had exercised over their daughter: "But I can see that the Marchioness was formed *at home,* before she mingled with the world; and I find she is continually operated upon by the correspondence of yourself and Mrs. Böhl. What a delight it must be to you to have children who richly repay you for all that you have implanted in their hearts and minds."[22]

Important as these thoughts about Fernán Caballero as a woman are in any biographical outline, the literary relationships, better discussed in reference to the particular works, are more pertinent. Evidently, Irving and Doña Cecilia engaged in serious, lengthy conversations about their respective writing hopes; and the latter, from available facts, freely gave to the foreign guest ideas, stories, and plots for future publications. Aside from the personal value and the fascinating literary affinities, however, the friendship appears ephemeral and a momentary interest—perhaps again because of Irving's desire to retain Böhl von Faber's help and also because of his own major writings about Spain with which he was arduously struggling during this residence. No influence of Irving can be clearly detected in Fernán Caballero's works, and she did not mention the American writer in correspondence and published material, somewhat surprising in view of her frequent utilization of names and quotations from other literatures. Irving, likewise, failed to keep the friendship as no extant letters or other items survive. More surprising still, is the fact that Irving, returning to Spain from 1842 to 1846 as the American Minister in Madrid, did not renew the friendship and, it would seem, did not see Fernán Caballero during these official years. However, in fairness to Irving, his efforts as a diplomat kept him very busy; and his romanticism possibly did not want to risk seeing changed times and places so that, during this second residence, he did not even visit the Alhambra in Granada where he had lived so happily and about which he had written one of his most successful books. A more delicate explanation than the above thesis of the fleeting friendship may be the altered status and considerably reduced circumstances, with resultant social limitations, of the former Marquesa de Arco-Hermoso. If, indeed, this courteous consideration explains the question, then the value of the Washington Irving-Fernán Caballero contacts increases in terms of revelations and insights about the budding literary endeavors of the latter.

VIII *Señora Arrom de Ayala*

After the death of the Marqués de Arco-Hermoso, Doña Cecilia, with her sister Angela, toured Europe in the following year, 1836, visiting the countries of Portugal, France, Belgium, and England. It is clear that these years, according to all commentators and her correspondence, represented critical, emotional, and unhappy times for Fernán Caballero; and the main problem is the comprehension of this woman's psychological suffering. At the same time, the personal crises supply some important clues and evidence for the artistic enterprises of this woman, demonstrating her true character during these periods of agonizing decisions.

The episodes were surely traumatic, beginning with the abrupt end by her second husband's death of the happiest period of her life up to then—and for the rest of her life. Subsequent quarrels about the estate with the deceased husband's family, and the required legal complications thereby, noticeably disillusioned Fernán Caballero at this stage. Also, the financial security of the widow was not as strong as she probably believed beforehand because the balance of the accounts showed about 135,000 *reales*—and Böhl von Faber had given 200,000 *reales* as a dowry. Of course, the remaining sum of money was certainly an adequate source of support, even if Doña Cecilia could not continue to enjoy all the expenses she did previously. The European tour lifted her spirits greatly, and a few later sketches (a reaction to a visit to Waterloo, for instance) show that she was profiting wisely by the necessary vacation abroad.

In England, however, occurred the only *gran amor* of Fernán Caballero, which ended sadly in her realization that the young English noble, identified by letters as "Federico Cuthbert," was interested in seduction rather than marriage.[23] Doña Cecilia's unhappiness was further compounded when, upon returning to Spain, she became aware that social circles were gossiping about her personal experiences in England. Ironically, Doña Frasquita had talked too freely about her daughter's interest in Cuthbert; and Doña Cecilia, after a tearful protest to her mother, expressed an age-old complaint in a letter about "my mother who has never loved me."[24] Böhl von Faber's death in the same year as the frustrated love affair with Cuthbert added a deep blow to Doña Cecilia's spirit; and Doña Frasquita's death, two years afterward, and after the above-mentioned friction between mother and daughter, struck a third cruel cut by death to the fabric of her emotions. In three years, Doña Cecilia's whole existence had been undermined by a series of unfortunate experiences, deaths, and unusual circumstances.

The most unusual circumstance, however, of this brief period of years was the marriage of Doña Cecilia to Antonio Arrom de Ayala on August 17, 1837. The fact of a third marriage for the widow—two years and five months to the day after the death of the Marqués de Arco-Hermoso—raised many uncharitable eyebrows in the conservative social circles of Andalucía, frequented by Doña Cecilia; and reports of the Cuthbert story provided further attention, undoubtedly. But, certainly, the most astonishing news about this third marriage was the identity of the bridegroom because Arrom de Ayala was only twenty-three years old and Doña Cecilia was now almost forty-one. Her third husband, of whom very little is still known, was apparently a delicate, artistic (and probably romantic) person; and he evidently pursued Doña Cecilia persistently until she consented to marry him.

Why did Doña Cecilia agree to this third marriage? The mystery has been discussed in generous terms by all critics, early and recent, and a general explanation has been accepted that compassion, as a first reason, influenced Doña Cecilia. Likewise, the fact that no children were born from any of the three marriages may have aroused maternal instincts in her, which she now saw realized in Arrom de Ayala.[25] Other conclusions have been advanced about the psychological and emotional state of the woman in 1837—reeling from one personal tragedy after another in very rapid succession. Surely, then, the events between 1835 and 1837 cannot be ignored in any effort to probe the motives for this third marriage. In addition, it seems possible to admit other conclusions, based on the background, writings, and correspondence of Fernán Caballero. Because of her exceptional education abroad and the cultural interests of the parents, Doña Cecilia, at this time, may have strongly felt the need to assert her personal independence and her status as a woman—ideas encountered in her works at later dates. The example of Doña Frasquita, despite any disagreement between mother and daughter, had established for Doña Cecilia the issue of feminism. Perhaps now, as a reaction and a challenge to the criticisms of Andalusian society (so cool after the death of the marquis to his previously welcomed widow) about the Cuthbert affair, Doña Cecilia, without the need to think of her father's views and perhaps as an answer to her mother's unfortunate words, called attention to herself as an individual and as a woman.

Her independence, or at least her action, nevertheless, did not lead to an easier life. Arrom de Ayala, whom she defended, encouraged, and helped faithfully, failed miserably in business matters; and the finances of Doña Cecilia, provided him without questions by her, were depleted by his bad luck and lack of business acumen. Her letters, however, show a constant love, whatever the roots of her feelings may be, for her third husband, who also was devoted to her in turn. The mounting financial problems resulted in long separations of the couple: Arrom de Ayala in 1840 went on an extended commercial trip to the Philippine Islands; and in 1853, he was appointed Spanish consul in Sydney, Australia, where he hoped also to recoup his losses through business enterprises. Arrom de Ayala's more or less definitive return in 1858 to Spain, where Fernán Caballero had achieved popularity and critical success, seemed, in turn, to mark a better period for him with advantageous prospects through investments for the future. His health, always uncertain with frequent illnesses, was matched by a sensitive temperament, which Doña Cecilia understood fully. Perhaps the rise and fall of his hopes so suddenly explain Arrom de Ayala's suicide in London on March 14, 1859, where he had gone in the expectation of very favorable business negotiations and had instead discovered that, somehow, he was almost totally ruined financially.

This loss of a third husband so tragically compelled Fernán Caballero to look inward and to consider seriously a retreat to a convent from the world—from the world which, in 1859, was greeting enthusiastically her writings. It is important to keep in mind that Fernán Caballero, deeply religious, must have been shocked not only by the suicide of Arrom de Ayala as her husband, but also by his fate, theologically. Ironically, Fernán Caballero, throughout her works, defended constantly and wholeheartedly the doctrines of the Catholic Church. The realization, then, that her husband had, by his suicide, condemned himself to an eternity in hell, according to her firmly held orthodoxy (even accepting the vague consolation that mental aberrations may be extenuating factors), placed Fernán Caballero in an agonizing dilemma between beliefs and sentiments. Fate had again dealt her a heart-rending blow, personal and professional;

and literature, a source of strength and expression, failed to sustain her in 1859 for continued successes as in the past.

IX   A Masculine World, a Masculine Name

Before 1849, the *annus mirabilis* of Fernán Caballero, her literary efforts and achievements can be divided into two phases, influenced clearly by her personal life: the happy years as the Marquesa de Arco-Hermoso, 1822-1835, when she gathered materials from her residences in Andalucía and began to rework the sources into literary form; and the years, 1835-1849, when she decided to publish essays at first and then short stories, leading to the novels of the "wonderful year." Doubt and conjecture still characterize the precise work of Fernán Caballero during the first period; but considerable endeavors were started at least, proved by the drafts of *La familia de Alvareda* and other tales available principally through the evidence of Washington Irving. The second period, again a period of accumulation and gestation, is initiated definitively with *La madre o El combate de Trafalgar* (*The Mother or the Battle of Trafalgar*), a short story published in *El Artista* in 1835 and signed "C. B." Apparently, Doña Frasquita translated the story into Spanish and pressed for publication—against her daughter's wishes and enthusiasm. The reasons for this apparent shyness may be glimpsed in the editorial note before the text, explaining that the author is *una señora* and that the absence of women writers in Spain gives "new luster to the positive merit of the following composition."[26] Already, the need, modesty, or fear of prejudice is apparent in Doña Cecilia's use of initials (correct, however) and her insistence upon anonymity. Doña Frasquita's role in her daughter's first publication was surely in keeping with her previous feminism—and indicates her influence and example for Fernán Caballero in 1849.

By 1840, after five years of emotional instabilities, Doña Cecilia submitted *Sola* (*Alone*) to a German magazine, which printed the short story in that language; and the most logical explanation would seem to be the existence of this magazine in Hamburg— a city with which she was intimately connected. Before 1845, she was writing more short stories, evidently now in French, and some irony is evident in her use of languages other than

Spanish for these first literary undertakings. It has been observed that Doña Cecilia, exposed to German, French, and Spanish during her educational experiences, home training, and residences was perhaps victimized by these exposures in that she was fluent but unpolished in the three languages.[27] Whatever the truth or cruelty of these observations may be, Doña Cecilia, after so many years in Spain, still preferred in her first major works to compose in French. Thus, by 1845, she was preparing *La Gaviota* (*The Sea Gull*) in French and claimed that *Elia* was already written in the same language. Aside from the nebulous state of the problems about the composition, completion, and final forms of several works, the importance of these years resides in the admission that Doña Cecilia was writing actively and in quantity. Her decision to embark upon a public career as a writer has been usually judged a necessary measure to relieve the growing financial distress caused after 1837 by the business disasters of Arrom de Ayala.[28] But the possibility of sublimation has been suggested for her needs and energies in view of the prolonged absences of her third husband from Spain. However, the inner ambitions of Doña Cecilia—clearly noted by Washington Irving a decade earlier—cannot be left aside as a primary motivation. In short, Doña Cecilia became Fernán Caballero because she had long wanted to be a writer; and present difficult circumstances, in addition to past and present encouragements, led to the embarrassing requests of editors and critics for their help—embarrassing because she was a woman and was cognizant all too well of her parental and personal associations. It has been surmised, for example, that Arrom de Ayala played a part in seeking publication for his wife's stories; but these suggestions are difficult to accept—or perhaps to reject—because of lack of knowledge about his life. Also, his trips and sojourns abroad might seem to rule against any outstanding role in Doña Cecilia's submissions and acceptances of manuscripts after 1845.

Her determined course of action, whatever may be the accuracy of a single theory or all viewpoints, was certainly finalized in 1848 because Doña Cecilia, in a letter to her father's gallant foe of the Calderonian Quarrel, José Joaquín de Mora, asked to send him *The Sea Gull* for publication: "Too much modesty or too much pride has prevented me from giving them (i.e., the pages of *The Sea Gull*) to anyone to read since the death of my parents, whose enthusiastic approval was, as you can imagine, my whole encouragement, eagerness, happiness, and compensation; but, lacking them, and urged by relatives and husband, I have decided to try giving them to the public," and "I shall send you one of my novels, illustrated by my husband's beautiful sketches, which give it great merit."[29] If these gentle requests, stimulated by the combined forces of Doña Cecilia's family and appreciation of her parents' devotion, failed to get acceptance from Mora because of the latter's busy schedule, Juan Eugenio Hartzenbusch's intervention caused Mora not only to accept *The Sea Gull* but, generously, to translate the text from French to Spanish. Hartzenbusch, wholeheartedly devoted to the Romantic Movement as a dramatist and critic, knew Doña Cecilia through his friendship with Böhl von Faber, whose library he had been negotiating to purchase for the Biblioteca Nacional in Madrid. Hartzenbusch's help and sympathy for Fernán Caballero continued in many ways during the following years, and his correspondence with her is, of course, an important example of the esteem in which she was held by her contemporaries.

The Sea Gull appeared in serial form in *El Heraldo*, the Madrid newspaper, from May 9th until July 9th of 1849. This "original novel of Spanish customs," according to the subtitle, won immediate popular success so that Fernán Caballero's stories, by the end of 1849, were indeed the first best sellers of modern Spanish literature. *El Heraldo* published in 1849, beginning on September 7th, *La familia de Alvareda,* and, on September 28th, *Una en otra* (*One in Another*); *Semanario Pintoresco Español* (*Spanish Picturesque Weekly*) published *Peso de un poco de paja* (*Burden of a Little Straw*), *Los dos amigos* (*The Two Friends*), *Sola* (*Alone*), and *La suegra del diablo* (*The Devil's Mother-in-Law*); *La España* (*Spain*) published *Elia*; and *La Ilustración* published *La hija del sol* (*The Daughter of the Sun*). Some of the overwhelming acclaim for these novels and stories, without detracting in any way from their intrinsic merit, may have been due to the astute decision to publish quickly—within less than one year—so many works. Logically, the public and critical reaction would be that a new, prolific writer had at last appeared on the rather bleak literary scene. However, the principal attraction resided in the subjects of the stories, a decisive break with the prevailing Romantic currents.

Who was Fernán Caballero? Part of the appeal for the new
author undoubtedly fell on the pseudonym selected by her;
curiosity to know the name of this woman who could challenge
so skillfully the masculine world of literature led to heightened
interest. Mora, in his announcement in *El Heraldo* of the coming publication of *The Sea Gull*, had utilized the pen name to
call attention to the author; and Eugenio de Ochoa, in a prestigious review of *La Gaviota* in August of 1849, referred to the
curiosity natural to anyone interested in the works of Fernán
Caballero, "un Walter Scott español."[30] This exuberant praise of
Ochoa, especially his conclusion that *The Sea Gull* would be the
Waverley of Spanish literature, represents Fernán Caballero's
definitive arrival on the literary scene—and is still a sound critical
analysis of the novel. The mystery of Fernán Caballero's choice
of the pen name has been challenged by some recent scholarship,
mainly because of the doubts about other facts of Coloma's
Recuerdos (*Remembrances*). However, the usual account is
certainly worthwhile quoting for an example of Fernán Caballero's *costumbrismo* and recognition of her mood:

I picked up some newspapers which were on the table in order
to look for any name at all that, appearing in public embarrassment,
could avoid being my own, and I found the report of a murder committed in a little town of La Mancha called Fernán Caballero.... I
liked this name because of its old and chivalric flavor, and without
hesitating a moment I sent it to Madrid, exchanging for the public,
my modest skirts of Cecilia for the very Spanish trousers of Fernán
Caballero.[31]

X *Literary Success*

Whatever the truth behind the selection of "Fernán Caballero"
as a literary pseudonym, the identity of Doña Cecilia was soon
revealed, probably as a slip of the tongue by Mora, because the
constant questions, guesses, and probings must have led to an
annoying time for Mora and Hartzenbusch, the two friends who
knew the name of the woman behind the façade of the writer.
She spoke bitterly at first of Mora's revelation because, in her
view, the distinction existed between the public figure and the
private individual; and she hoped to keep separate the writer
and the woman, Fernán Caballero and Cecilia Böhl de Faber, as

two very different persons.[32] Her theory, then, of femininity contrasts sharply with the overt example of her mother and very interestingly with the cases of her European contemporaries, George Eliot and George Sand. A comparison suggested during her life between Fernán Caballero and George Sand brought an indignant denial from the former. Fernán Caballero's defense of femininity is the defense of the Spanish woman against the trends of blatant displays in public. Nevertheless, the continued literary successes of Fernán Caballero during the ten years, 1849-1859, provided the first highly important and influential entrance of a woman on the stage of modern Spanish literature.

Within the framework of her insistence on the divorce between the writer and the woman, Fernán Caballero took pride in her literary victories against the usual pattern of masculine domination. Her modesty, on the contrary, won respect and admirers; and her achievements as a writer brought concomitant admiration as a person. In 1850, she published *Lágrimas, No transige la conciencia* (*No Compromise with Conscience*) and *La noche de navidad* (*Christmas Night*) in *El Heraldo; Callar en vida y perdonar en muerte* (*Silence in Life and Pardon in Death*), *El ex-voto* (*The Ex-Vow*), *El albañil* (*The Mason*), *El marinero* (*The Sailor*), and *El sochantre* (*The Subchanter*) in *La España; Un quid pro quo* (*A Tit for Tat*), *Los caballeros del pez* (*The Gentlemen of the Fish*), and *El vendedor de tagarninas* (*The Oyster Plant Seller*) in *Semanario Pintoresco Español*. An ironic success also came in the same year when a pirated edition of *La familia de Alvareda*, copied verbatim from *El Heraldo*, appeared in *La Crónica* (*The Chronicle*) of New York City. In 1851, her output decreased somewhat: *Los escoberos* (*The Broomsellers*), *Con mal o con bien a los tuyos te ten* (*Stay with your Own in Good and Bad*), *Matrimonio bien avenido, la mujer junto al marido* (*In a Harmonious Marriage, the Wife Is at the Side of her Husband*), *El Eddistone* (*The Eddystone*) in *Semanario Pintoresco Español*; and *La hija del sol* (*The Daughter of the Sun*) as a separate volume. In 1852, *Clemencia* and *Cuadros de costumbres populares andaluces* (*Popular Andalusian Local Color Sketches*) were the principal offerings in addition to *Lucas García*, issued separately, and three short tales in *Semanario Pintoresco Español*. In 1853, a corrected edition of *Lágrimas,* and the stories *Simón Verde* and *Más largo es el tiempo que la fortuna (Time Is Longer than Fortune),* were the publications.

In 1855, the first effort at the *Obras completas* was initiated by Mellado in Madrid, which was finished in 1858 for a total of nineteen volumes. The shift to a compilation of her works, rather than the successive publication in magazines of stories and novels, represented for Fernán Caballero a source of complaints about the slowness and queries of editors and publishers. This concentration upon an early "complete works" also signified that she had really utilized the main resources of her literary art, stored away during an earlier period, especially as the Marquesa de Arco-Hermoso. Although, in 1855, Fernán Caballero will still publish *La Estrella de Vandalia (The Star of Vandalia), Justa y Rufina, Las dos gracias (The Two Graces), Tres almas de Dios (Three Souls of God),* the first title of *Un servilón y un liberalito (A Loyalist and a Liberal),* and apparently an edition of *Un verano en Bornos (A Summer in Bornos),* the prolific days since *La Gaviota* are over. Nevertheless, by 1857, Fernán Caballero was established in the public and critical mind as a major writer of the century. Her financial plight, of course, was known to friends and various influential circles, such as the Duke and Duchess of Montpensier, because of the misfortunes of Arrom de Ayala; and a residence in the Alcázar of Sevilla, provided by Queen Isabel II in recognition and friendship, solved for Fernán Caballero in 1857 the problem of her finances. Ironically but happily in this year of decreased publications, European regard for her work spread abroad the name of Fernán Caballero: Antoine de Latour devoted a long essay to her in the French review, *Le Correspondant,* in 1857; Ferdinand Wolf in 1859 published in German a study on the Realistic novel in Spain, mentioning her very favorably; and *The Edinburgh Review* in 1861 noted that "the appearance therefore of an author like Fernán Caballero, a really original writer of fiction ... is an event in the literary history of Spain, and we may even add, in that of Europe ... it is certain that no living writer has shed so bright a lustre on Spanish literature."[33]

Fernán Caballero, around 1853, had started to dedicate many hours to extensive correspondence, another reason, perhaps, for her failure or inability to sustain the pace of publication since the "wonderful year" of 1849. However, the letters of Fernán Caballero, although they were written many years after the inception and drafts of her ideas, have been recognized not only as a valid source for the understanding of the writer, but likewise for a fascinating psychological study of the woman. Indeed, she has been called a most important example of the epistolary art in Spanish literature, and her letters are worthy companions for those of Madame de Staël.[34] Writing was obviously a vocation but also an outlet for the many unlucky circumstances of her life as, for example, in one revelation she said: "In the many and grave afflictions that God has sent me, they consoled me, creating for me a world of fiction and remembrances in which I withdrew as into parentheses."[35] She also spoke in letters of her ideas about literature and explained very forcefully her theories on the novel—her novel—as the vehicle of artistic, philosophical, and ideological arguments. In short, the letters of Fernán Caballero, when analyzed as a whole, lead to the important conclusion that her works were more than an effort to gain money, fame, and inner satisfaction. Many years before Realism in Spain, and very close to the Realistic period in France of Balzac (whom she admired), Fernán Caballero had conceived a successful formula against the prevailing and excessive currents of a Romanticism as a revolt rather than as a revival. The question has been raised that Fernán Caballero, if she had published earlier and had publicized more her theories, might rank as one of the truly influential European Realists, especially in view of the appreciation of her work shortly after 1849.

IX *The Sad Years*

These comments and regrets[36] add to the tragedy, still a major factor of Fernán Caballero's life, of the years after 1857. The suicide of her third husband so overwhelmed the distraught widow that she tried to withdraw completely from the world by planning to live permanently in a convent, an idea rejected as unwise by friends and religious advisers. Nevertheless, after Arrom de Ayala's death in 1859, her association was restricted increasingly to individuals of long acquaintance or trusted friendship. She became annoyed by the many visitors, Spanish and foreign, who wanted, perhaps out of curiosity and at times from enthusiastic interest, to discuss with Spain's most prominent novelist the ideas and theories of her work. Thus, at the moment when she enjoyed most popularity, influence, and prestige, Fernán Caballero took no part in the novelistic directions she had implemented in her writings for almost ten years. Through the limited extension of the correspondence, she explained her philosophy of literature and the novel as, for instance, in the thesis of her art as "the poetization of truth."[37]

As a writer, consequently, her work was essentially terminated; and these years from 1857 until 1877 require no extensive investigations as do the earlier years before 18). In 1857, the publication of Relaciones, Cuadros de costumঞes, and Lady Virginia continue the Obras completas or are minor endeavors; in 1858, the complete edition of Mellado is still valid because only a few brief pieces in journals add to the total output; in 1859, the final form of Un servilón y un liberalito and the completion of collaboration with a magazine, La Educación Pintoresca (The Picturesque Education), as well as another collection of Cuentos y poesías populares andaluces (Popular Andalusian Short Stories and Poems) marked this tragic year for Fernán Caballero. After 1860, in fact, the sole noteworthy novel is La farisea (The Woman of the Pharisees), published in 1863 in La Concordia (Concord), but which, in 1865, reached at least four editions. It became perhaps her best-selling novel. Ironically, the popularity of Fernán Caballero continued and increased during these declining years of small literary productions and personal unhappiness. A new try at the Obras completas by Mellado, started in 1861 and finished in 1864, reached sixteen volumes. One year later, in 1865, a third edition of the Obras completas was initiated by the Madrid house of Sáenz de Jubera, which, curiously, did not reach the fourteenth, and last, volume until 1893. Nevertheless, the decade from 1860 until 1870, in general terms, represents a time of further attention and publication (in the established form of complete works) for Fernán Caballero, although she had clearly by now exhausted the storehouse of her literary materials. The period of her works, covering the political and social events of Romanticism, the reign of Fernando VII, and the first years of Isabel II, no longer found continuation and development in the few important endeavors after 1857.

Another facet of Fernán Caballero's popularity as a writer, after the influential praise of foreign critics in journals and reviews, was the noticeable increase in translations abroad after 1857 and very discernible by 1863. The most prestigious diffusion in Europe, or at least the most extensive publication beyond Spain, was the inclusion of her works in the *Colección de Autores Españoles* (*Collection of Spanish Authors*) by F. A. Brockhaus of Leipzig, Germany. The translations into French, however, of Fernán Caballero's novels and short stories seemingly stand out as the most numerous; and, as for individual books, *The Family of Alvareda* gradually emerges as the most popular publication, not only in France but in the other countries where translations and editions have been traced. England, for example, saw in 1861 a two-volume set, including *Elia* and *The Family of Alvareda,* under the imaginative title of *The Castle and the Cottage in Spain* by Lady Wallace. In the United States, *The Sea Gull* was translated in 1864 and *Elia or Spain Fifty Years Ago* in 1868. The pattern of early and continued renditions of Fernán Caballero's writings is clearly established throughout the European and American scenes so that she is, unquestionably, the first Spanish author of the nineteenth century who repeatedly and successfully crossed the cultural barrier of the Pyrenees for an international audience.[38]

These foreign successes, nevertheless, did not always please Fernán Caballero although, of course, her feelings were mixed between pride and fear: pride for the recognition of herself as a writer and a woman, and fear that foreigners would misinterpret her nation. Supposedly, Washington Irving had wanted to translate into English *The Family of Alvareda* when he first read the story in 1829, and Fernán Caballero had gently refused permission because she did not consider that this novel was correctly representative of Spanish life, especially for foreigners. Ironically, then, the fact that this novel was preferred by translators must have vexed her.[39] But contemporary criticism, which in many instances still prefers *The Family of Alvareda* as the most significant book of Fernán Caballero, shows perhaps that her anxieties and complaints were not justified and that the literary, psychological features of this novel raise the place of her

contributions—and Spain's—to literature. Also, by the time of
these foreign versions, the Spanish novel after 1870, and particularly 1874, with Galdós, Valera, and Alarcón, was developing
beyond Fernán Caballero's influential achievements from 1849
until 1857.

By 1868, Fernán Caballero as a force in literature was disappearing from critical attention when, in that year, because
of the revolution and consequent abdication of Isabel II, the
nearly destitute writer lost the comfortable residence in the
Alcázar given her by a grateful Queen. The political conservatism of Fernán Caballero, expressed repeatedly and uncompro-
misingly in novels such as *Elia* and *Un servilón y un liberalito*,
encountered powerful opponents in the crises between 1868
and 1875. The many publishing successes, in Spain and abroad,
evidently brought her no financial gains through circumstances
still not clearly explained. On the contrary, her desperate finances
from 1849 until 1859, the decade of emotional rather than rational
investments in Arrom de Ayala's enterprises, declined addition-
ally after his suicide; and the following decade, despite Isabel
II's gift of a home in 1857 and popular favor from readers, witnessed sporadic embarrassments about money—a long journey
from the years as the Marquesa de Arco-Hermoso. Finally, then,
the last years were spent in retirement in Sevilla in the most
humble circumstances, a humiliating eclipse, almost impossible
for her to endure at times, beyond the hardships already suffered in the previous twenty years, 1849-1868.

The miserable years between 1868 and 1875 depressed almost
hopelessly the aging woman because of the fall of the monarchy
and the apparent triumph of the liberals, or those elements she
opposed consistently in her writings. Her friends in high places
no longer counted in the topsy-turvy atmosphere of government;
and, indeed, some were compelled to live abroad during this
chaotic era of political instability. The few small items Fernán
Caballero sent for publication were printed without much fan-
fare and with less reaction, and her prestige went into swift decline because of the unpopular ideas she had defended previously
in her apogee. The collapse of republican or liberal theories in
the practical arena of politics proved her correct, in her firmly
held view, but, obviously, these failures darkened her last years
because of the harm done to Spain, always uppermost in

her aesthetic vision. Finally, the restoration of the Bourbons at the end of 1875, with Alfonso XII, son of Isabel II, as the king, revived Fernán Caballero's spirits during her final months. During these concluding months of her life, she saw the return of the traditions encouraged in her works, even though this Bourbon revival met with much opposition from the Realistic novelists such as Galdós, and soon the Naturalists, who had followed at first and then had traveled past the literary signposts erected securely against Romanticism by Fernán Caballero. Her personal circumstances, while not improved a great deal, were at least ameliorated by the restored fortunes of friends among royalist circles. The Duke and Duchess of Montpensier, whose secretary, Antoine de Latour, had enhanced Fernán Caballero's prestige through his articles, renewed their friendship and help. This aristocratic couple and the former Queen, Isabel II, paid visits to Fernán Caballero shortly before her death in Sevilla on April 7, 1877.[40]

By 1877, however, the Realists no longer accepted Fernán Caballero's novelistic doctrines for the most part; and the defects in her literary and ideological vision detracted from any strict imitations, although, of course, the main forms of her theories blended with the regionalism characteristic of many novels during the second half of the century. Nevertheless, her innovative contributions, never challenged seriously despite the ideological differences during the turbulent years between Isabel II and Alfonso XII, were respected by the leading novelists such as Galdós and Valera, even if they disagreed with aesthetic points and indicated overtly the disadvantages of her novelistic art. The critics, such as Marcelino Menéndez Pelayo, also lent support to the respect accorded Fernán Caballero. Her death, in fact, drew immediately national honors and the acceptance, reminiscent of the "wonderful year," 1849, and up to 1857, by the literary establishment of an assured place in modern Spanish literature, a place secured up to the present, though downgraded harshly on occasions. And, obviously, Fernán Caballero's importance in the national literature was correctly first recognized because of the publication of *La Gaviota* in 1849, the initiation and the winning example of a new novel.

CHAPTER 2

A Model for the Modern Novel

IN 1849 the popular and critical success of *La Gaviota* (*The Sea Gull*), immediate and overwhelming, brought acceptance of the book as the initial triumph of the modern novel in Spanish literature, an opinion still accepted by literary historians. The plethora of Spanish translations of European novels during the first half of the nineteenth century reflected the acceptance of foreign influences; and the few worthwhile native contributions, such as Gil y Carrasco's *El señor de Bembibre* (*The Lord of Bembibre*) in 1844, utilized Romantic devices in general or with slight variations.[1] A novel, then, taking place in Spain with recognizable Spanish settings, characters, and descriptions provided a very different contribution, especially with the time shifted from the usual medieval, Romantic ambiances to the contemporary period and, indeed, to the year, 1848, when *The Sea Gull* ends. Of course, the European novelists, Balzac and Dickens, had employed the present rather than the past as a cornerstone of their Realistic doctrines; but the corresponding Spanish novel of Realism, or at least the beginnings of Realism, had to await the publication of *The Sea Gull*. In addition, Fernán Caballero advanced the theory as well as the practice of the modern Spanish novel by the prologue to her novel, later added to the book version, but an accepted guide to her ideas at the time of composition and serial publication.

I A Novel of Customs

This brief, succinct prologue to *The Sea Gull* is also a direct, precise statement of Fernán Caballero's aims and is likewise an important manifesto of the definitive break between Romanticism and Realism. The terminology, however, is expressed as the distinction between a "novel" and a "novel of customs"; but the differences are clearly stated, revealing thereby a firm under-

46

standing of the new orientation for this genre. She is, in fact, wary about the use of the word "novel" to classify *The Sea Gull* because *la novela* is evidently associated too closely with Romanticism for her; and the novel is likewise synonymous with the imagination, in her view. The *novela de costumbres*, then, will not emphasize the prominent features of the Romantic novel so that imagination and the plot, or the intrigue, are relegated to minor roles in the construction of *The Sea Gull*.

Instead of utilizing the Romantic formulae of a complicated, exotic plot and giving free rein to imaginative treatment of the story, Fernán Caballero somewhat modestly claims that it is only necessary "to compile and to copy" in order to compose the new novel, such as *The Sea Gull*. Observation opposed to imagination, truth opposed to invention, led logically to the need of the novel being set in the present and in Spain where the two criteria were at first hand for the writer. Characters also existed in the rural and urban social strata although Fernán Caballero does not claim that all her characters are so directly sketched. For example, she moves forward in the direction of character studies when she writes that the actors in her drama of *The Sea Gull* are neither totally good or perfect, nor are they completely evil, as in melodramas, referring to the Romantic theater. Fernán Caballero, in her acceptance of the Balzacian idea,[2] attempts to indicate the "characteristic trait" of the personages, creating of course types, but at the same time individual persons.

However, Fernán Caballero interrupted these thoughts on the art of *The Sea Gull* by analyzing her countrymen honestly and frankly, and also by defending the Spaniard against the criticism of foreigners. No contradiction exists in these apparently distinct treatments, and she is very perceptive about the national temperament, after the previous probes of Larra, before the extensive critiques of Galdós, and yet relevant for any understanding of the future problem for the Generation of 1898. Fernán Caballero places her countrymen in four classes: the vociferous defenders of the national tradition who refuse to admit adverse comments, except in the political sphere; the fawning imitators of foreign models, refusing to consider anything Spanish to be worthwhile; the irrational advocates of a Spain already enjoying the best of all possible worlds; and the fourth group, representing the majority of Spaniards (including Doña Cecilia, as she insists),

who favor an eclectic approach by accepting slowly and gradually any foreign ideas. This last class first weighs change
from abroad against a scrutiny of present conditions and only
makes modifications if these new approaches are in accord with
the Spanish or native character. In short, the analysis and understanding of *lo castizo*, the purely Spanish, must take place before
European developments are admitted; but the Pyrenees certainly
provides no ideological, philosophical, or social barrier to national
progress. These views of Fernán Caballero, similar to Unamuno's
ideas at the beginning of *En torno al casticismo* (*On the Problem
of Spanishness*), are of course essentially moderate and conservative; but the tone is encouraging at this critical direction of
Spanish life and literature in the second half of the nineteenth
century.

These theories of the prologue are reinforced within *The Sea
Gull* during the discussions in the second part at the social
gatherings in Sevilla and Madrid, where Fernán Caballero also
attempts "to give an exact, true and genuine idea of Spain"
and where "the European public might have a correct idea of
Spain and of Spaniards," as she states in the prologue. This
defense of Spaniards against foreign misinterpretations and harsh
criticisms is of course interesting in view of Fernán Caballero's
parentage and her own extensive residence abroad, including the
present problem of the original version of *The Sea Gull* in
French as a language in which, apparently, she wrote more
easily than in Spanish.[3] She even seems a little strident in her
opinion that foreigners have consistently misinterpreted the
Spanish character and scene, and that her compatriots have
not corrected the European image of Spain by their own
explanations. Also, this desire for a truthful, accurate foreign
opinion serves as some argument for the favorable picture of
rural life, customs, and characters, especially in the first part of
The Sea Gull.

II *A Romantic Plot*

Structurally, *The Sea Gull* is a better-organized novel than
critics have recognized or accepted. It has two parts of almost
equal length, with fifteen and sixteen chapters, respectively,
and with the action occurring first in the country and next in

the city, the division into two parts clearly indicating this change of place. The first and final chapters, shifting quickly and sharply in time and place, comprise perhaps the form of a prologue and an epilogue for the story. The year is immediately indicated in the beginning of both these chapters, 1836 and 1848, but the plot really starts in the second chapter, two years later, in 1838 with the traditional, realistic employment of time in chronological, linear manner. And, in fact, Fernán Caballero generally inserts without delay in each chapter the time and place of the events she is about to narrate.[4]

In the first chapter, a chance meeting between two young men, a German doctor and a Spanish duke, on board an English ship heading for Spain, results in an immediate friendship between these apparently different but, in reality, similar travelers. Fritz Stein is the epitome of German Romanticism, and the Duke of Almansa is the symbol of Spanish chivalry; the former is the noblest representative of foreigners, and the latter is the best example of native aristocracy. The physician, encouraged and helped by the generous Spaniard, explains his choice of an incongruous career: service with the army in Spain in the humanitarian aim of alleviating the sufferings of the wounded. Stein's mission, quixotic and romantic, is tinged with a trace of melancholy, caused by the loneliness and vagueness of his decision to go to Spain, about which he knows nothing.

Two years later, in the second chapter, Stein appears broken in spirit and in body because of his bitter experiences in war; he had charitably and as a medical officer treated a wounded soldier from the opposing Carlist forces, with the result that he was thrown out of the army. A culminating blow of misfortune occurs when Treu, his faithful dog, sacrifices himself to protect the master from the charge of a wild bull. Stein's breakdown takes place when he, romantically, sheds copious tears and arrives at the top of a height where a magnificent view of sea, setting sun, the ruins of a fort, and a monastery encourages him to hasten to possible help. He is rescued, after fainting, by two residents, Brother Gabriel and Aunt María, who, with the latter's daughter, Dolores, and her husband, Manuel, decide to nurse the stranger.

Stein's recovery, proceeding rapidly with the simple, effective measures of the family, is also encouraged by his walks around the countryside near the village of Villamar, where his depression and bitter experiences are erased by the scenery and the people. His visits to the monastery, abandoned and in ruins, and to Fort St. Christopher, symbols of the two pillars of Spanish glories, the Church and the Sword, with their respective representatives, Brother Gabriel and Don Modesto Guerrero, move Stein to an understanding and respect for Spanish traditions and life. The uncomplicated daily lives of the people of Villamar, with their reliance upon folklore and stories, please the German physician so that he is now content to remain here forever.

In the eighth chapter, at the halfway point of this first part, Stein meets Marisalada, the daughter of the fisherman, Pedro Santaló; and he is able to repay his hosts for their care and kindnesses by prescribing the proper treatment for the consumptive girl, who is, however, haughty and unappreciative. Her singing has earned her the nickname of "Sea Gull" or *Gaviota* from Momo, the unruly, sharp-tongued grandson of the kindly Aunt María. Pedro Santaló is persuaded to allow Marisalada to live with Aunt María so that she can be provided the medical attention of Stein and the necessary personal attention of the family. Stein, fully recovered, marvels at the changes in Marisalada, especially the girl's talented singing, after a short period in the home of his own hosts. However, Marisalada is troublesome at school and flirts with Ramón Pérez, the barber's son, to the dismay of Mystical Rose, the schoolmistress.

Three years pass quietly and happily for Stein in Villamar where, however, he has been slowly falling in love with his former patient and present music pupil, Marisalada. Aunt María, cognizant of his love and alert to the advantages of having a resident doctor in the village, actively promotes the match; but Stein, emphasizing the age difference, since he is twenty-nine and Marisalada is sixteen, shyly pleads the impossibility of marriage. But under Aunt María's tutelage, Stein does begin to pay court to Marisalada who, likewise, has been urged to accept Stein as a husband by the countrywoman. In a romantic, melodramatic scene, Stein proposes and Marisalada accepts, although her replies are unenthusiastic and brief to his ardent words. The wedding, of course, causes rejoicing in the village of Villamar, for Stein's sake rather than for Marisalada's unmerited good fortune, in the eyes of the realistic, perceptive common folk.

Three more years bring Stein further contentment and satisfaction, when fate intervenes in the appearance of the Duke of Almansa, badly hurt in a fall from a horse, and who, in appreciation of Stein's expert medical care, rewards the doctor and the villagers generously for their hospitality. Ironically, the duke, after hearing Marisalada sing, insists upon rewarding the couple by taking them to the city, away from the monotonous life of Villamar, where Stein's wife will be able to win acclaim for her artistry and the husband will secure a prestigious, profitable career as a physician. Marisalada is overjoyed at this great expectation and eagerly leaves the village; Stein is devastated by this unwanted change in his life; and the villagers, particularly Pedro Santaló, sadly watch the departure of Stein and Marisalada.

III   *A Realistic Turn*

Critics have been in agreement, beginning with Ochoa's view of *The Sea Gull*, that the second part is less interesting, less sympathetic in approach and characterization, and lacking in the warmth of the *costumbrista* sketches inserted frequently in the first part. These critical reactions represent probably the intention of Fernán Caballero because she downgrades the façades of society, the city, and the latest fashions that come generally from abroad; and it is natural that these tendencies appear reflected, consciously and perhaps subconsciously, throughout the second part.

The *tertulia* at the house of the Countess of Algar, a possible literary rendition of Fernán Caballero as the Marquesa de Arco-Hermoso, is marked by a gossipy, frivolous quality, with little direct importance for the plot. Stein and Marisalada, for instance, do not appear in this initial chapter of the second part, although the Duke of Almansa supplies the news about their arrival in the city of Sevilla. However, some interest is inherent in the light discussions as, for example, the mention of foreign opinions about the Spanish world; the chauvinism of Spaniards, such as General Santa María; the snobbism of some Spaniards, such as Eloísa; and the oblique references to the increasing problem of the polarization of Spanish politics, between the liberals and the traditionalists. But the action intensifies in the second chapter when the Duke of Almansa, intending to provide a spectacle for his friends, takes Stein and Marisalada to the bullfight. The episode is repugnant for Stein who flees the scene to enjoy the historic sights of Sevilla; but Marisalada's attraction toward Pepe Vera, the principal bullfighter, is totally dedicated, obvious even to the duke. The brutalities of the national sport are described in detail and with stress on the gory aspects, such as the slaughter of the horses.

The days in Sevilla, until the scene shifts in the eighth chapter to Madrid, provide little action beyond the confines of the parties, such as the *tertulia* at the beginning of this second division; and, indeed, the chapters are lacking in any major development of the main plot, minimized anyway, according to the novelistic ideas of Fernán Caballero. Nevertheless, the discussions about literary, political, and social topics contribute to the themes and contemporary quality of the story, detracting in no manner from the historical value of Fernán Caballero's work. As another explanation, the insistence of the author upon the minor role of any plots (since the plot is a pronounced Romantic trait) can be recalled in view of this slow-moving beginning of the second part.

When, however, the story is transferred to the capital, Marisalada in Madrid begins to emerge as the most important character of the novel, and the action is intensified, coming to a head with a bold topic in Spanish literature for this period: sex and adultery. It is curious that Fernán Caballero on several occasions opposed these topics as validly meritorious elements in a literary work, and Ochoa, in his review, looked unfavorably upon this turn in the plot.[5] The substitution, however, of a realistic, understandable portrayal of love and a wife's temptations is certainly more interesting than the previously described romantic, poetical speeches of Stein and his idealistic devotion to Marisalada. Ironically, then, Fernán Caballero has within these chapters in Madrid advanced immeasurably the direction—and future—of the Spanish novel. Marisalada, by the conclusion of the seventh chapter, is involved in an adulterous affair with Pepe Vera, and the novel has left the path of placid descriptions of local color scenes and society chatterings to travel a new road of tragic and human complications. In the European novel of George Eliot and George Sand, of course, the themes of sex, adultery, and illicit love were repeatedly employed as essential aspects of the story, integral to a substantial plot. Fernán Caballero, strongly against any critical resemblances to George Sand imposed by her contemporaries, utilized the same themes in other novels; and, indeed, her feminine characters are often marked by their freedom from social pressures and acceptable conduct in their married status.

The downfall of Marisalada starts in Madrid although, to all appearances, she is at the height of her artistic popularity and the object of devotion from the duke, Stein, and, of course, Pepe Vera. But the flaws in this heroine's (or antiheroine's) personality are becoming too obvious, too flagrant, and too distasteful; and all sympathy for her disappears for the reader. At least, in Villamar, excuses or explanations were possible because of the girl's illness, lack of a strong parental guidance, and an adolescent temperament; but now, Marisalada insults the Duchess of Almansa by ostentatious behavior, indicating the singer's influence over the duke, and the lack of courteous manners at receptions in noble homes is very apparent. If justice and morality are to triumph, then "The Sea Gull" must be punished; and Fernán Caballero illustrates this obvious desire on her part by the death of Pedro Santaló.

Momo, sent to Madrid by Aunt María, returns to Villamar after a humorous, unsuccessful visit to the city to see Marisalada and to inform the daughter about the parent's fatal decline. The poorly-endowed country bumpkin has been overwhelmed by the strange sights and activities of the busy metropolis. His interpretation of Marisalada's role on stage, where she is killed, is similar to Estanislao del Campo's gaucho in the Argentinian poem, *Fausto*, where the theatrical appearances are accepted as reality so that Momo—not too unhappily in view of his constant antipathy to "The Sea Gull"—reports to the village about his adventures and Marisalada's death. Pedro Santaló, comforted as best he can be by his friends, dies without having seen his daughter, whose supposed murder was not revealed to him. The scene of Santaló's dying moments, in the Romantic manner of melodramatic descriptions, utilizing a storm as the backdrop, is also a fervent defense, on the author's part, of the place of religion, orthodoxy, and tradition in the life and death of man.

These two chapters, the ninth and tenth, of Momo's excursion to Madrid and the death of Marisalada's father, exist independ-

ently from the main action of Marisalada, but the episodes are
morally and structurally related to the thematic purposes of
Fernán Caballero. There is no longer any doubt that, with
admirable skill, the author has compelled readers, realistic and
romantic, to arrive at the only fair, just conclusion that Marisalada now deserves punishment. Immediately, in the twelfth
chapter when the story is returned to Madrid and Marisalada
is the center of the plot, the collapse of the girl's world is effected.
Her disregard for Stein's admittedly very romantic though highly
admirable devotion is repaid by Pepe Vera's arrogant, heartless,
and essentially cruel reactions to Marisalada's passion. She
becomes a slave to the bullfighter's whims, and the consequences
can only be tragic as her health is neglected by a strenuous
career of singing, late hours, and parties.

Finally, Stein, alerted by a letter from a jilted girl friend of
Pepe Vera about Marisalada's adultery, discovers the truth
by following the clues in Lucía del Salto's embittered revelation.
The husband's faith and trust cannot survive the sight of Marisalada and Pepe Vera so that Stein, on the following day, explains
to the Duke of Almansa his intention to leave his faithless wife,
a course of action really advocated by the nobleman after hearing
the doctor's sad tale. The shock of Marisalada's unfaithfulness
also brings the duke to the realization that he has neglected his
own wife in his disguised hope of winning the love of "The Sea
Gull," and the duke at once pleads for the Duchess of Almansa
to forgive him. In fact, the noble family, reunited happily,
decides to leave Madrid—and Marisalada—for their home in
Andalucía.

Marisalada is unaware of the departures of her husband and
the duke, and she is coerced harshly by Pepe Vera to attend the
bullfight in which he will star that afternoon. Feverish and ill, the
girl attends the spectacle because she is afraid that her lover
would abandon her to return to Lucía del Salto. The bullfight,
where she first saw Pepe Vera, becomes the occasion for Marisalada's last, traumatic view of the bullfighter, gored fatally in
his attempt to conquer the prize bull of the afternoon. Alone
and deserted by everyone, Marisalada is very ill in her untidy,
barren house, robbed of everything possible by the unscrupulous
servants. The concluding irony for the moment is the appearance
of a nun, a Sister of Charity, to help the impoverished girl

because Marisalada, in the presence of the Duchess of Almansa at the latter's home, had previously resented the attention given to the same nun.

In the final two chapters, the scene shifts to familiar settings, first, at the salon of the Countess of Algar, and finally, at the village of Villamar. Six months have passed since Pepe Vera's death and Marisalada's illness, and the guests at the Countess of Algar's reception have almost forgotten the girl despite their previous enthusiasm for her talented singing. In several remarks, the well-deserved judgment of a just fate is assigned Marisalada for her arrogance, boorishness, and treatment of Stein. One of the guests, present at an earlier *tertulia,* has just returned from Cuba with news that Stein died of yellow fever there shortly after his arrival, characteristically helping his fellowmen. Stein, on his deathbed, had given Rafael, the cousin of the Countess, a letter for Marisalada. The Countess of Algar reads the poignant, brief message: "María, whom I have loved so much and whom I still love: if my forgiveness can save you any remorse, if my blessing can contribute to your happiness, then take them both from my deathbed" (I, 132). This concluding paragraph of the fifteenth chapter could have possibly ended the novel, and the story would have been complete, with Marisalada's future bleak and her early death, because of ill health, a logical result of her cruel, immoral behavior. This possibility for a conclusion would be in keeping with Romantic examples, such as *La Traviata,* and the didactic purposes of Fernán Caballero would have been served forcefully and acceptably, from the standard literary vogues. If, consequently, Fernán Caballero had decided to remain with the current Romantic literature, she could have stopped at this melodramatic point, the reading of Stein's letter.

However, the Realistic turn, by means of an additional chapter, almost in the form of an epilogue, adds effectively to the importance of *The Sea Gull* as the forerunner of Realism in Spain. At the same time, the artistic qualities are enhanced with humor, contemporary references, some further characterization, particularly with Momo, and an unforgettable, final portrait of Marisalada. "The Sea Gull" is not granted a Romantic, tragic death—morally deserved but still winning some measure of sympathy from tenderhearted audiences—and, instead, is given a life sentence of punishment as the wife of Ramón Pérez, the barber's son, whom she had previously scorned. In fact, Marisalada bears little resemblance to her former appearance in the drawing rooms of Sevilla and Madrid; she has lost her voice, is unkempt from overwork with children, household, and a domineering mate, and is finally no more than a shrew, living vainly on her few moments of glory in the past. Always ready to hurl his usual insult in her face is Momo, crude but effective in the refrain: "You were a Sea Gull, you are a Sea Gull, you will be a Sea Gull." The unpleasant connotations of the term, "Sea Gull," apply in Spanish usage to a woman lacking in delicate feminine manners and expressing herself loudly, vulgarly. Momo, no laudatory character from his first entrance into the novel, is nevertheless the spokesman for Fernán Caballero's didacticism and morality in this striking vignette of Marisalada, four years later, in 1848.

The ruins of time have also resulted in the end of the local color atmosphere of Villamar. Aunt María and Brother Gabriel have died; the fort, still under the command of the declining Don Modesto Guerrero, is closer to total collapse; and the signs of the nineteenth century are appearing in Villamar. The façades of democratic tendencies give the village a burlesque air, resented by all the citizens who, according to Fernán Caballero, yearn for the good old days of monarchy, church, and tradition. In short, Villamar, in 1848, the year of European revolutions, is no longer the happy, tranquil countryside of 1838 when Stein arrived. The strengths of Spanish life are being drained by alien doctrines, modes, and ideologies, namely the influences of eighteenth-century Enlightenment and nineteenth-century Liberalism; and Fernán Caballero, briefly but clearly, gives this final emphasis to these evils—a view encountered in her complete works with resounding repetition. She calls attention to a later novel, *Lágrimas*, a sequel to *The Sea Gull*, in that the action takes place in Villamar; some of the characters, such as Momo, appear again; and the problems of the new age are probed as a warning to the author's compatriots against the prevailing currents of the nineteenth century.

Thus, in the sixteenth chapter, Fernán Caballero has decidedly advanced her book beyond the limitations of the Romantic novel, and she has foreshadowed the issues investigated in the later, outstanding novels of Pérez Galdós. It is true that Fernán Caballero is no impartial observer of the contemporary scene of

1848; her sympathies are with the past, with the world before 1836, when Spain was suffering under the tyranny of Fernando VII. The value, then, of this last chapter is important as a literary solution to a novelistic venture, realistically and effectively, and as a realization of the confrontation between the city and the country, between the democratic spirit of the times and the yearning for the changeless, traditional ways, unfortunately, for the author, vanishing quickly.[6]

IV *Andalusian Local Color*

Fernán Caballero's aim to write a novel of customs is achieved through observation, a Realistic feature, but the selection of material is nonetheless subjected to her ideological beliefs: traditional, monarchical, Catholic, conformist. Her Realism is also placed at the service of her Romanticism about Spain so that the scenes are idealized, the favorable aspects of rural life are selected, and the characters are devoid of complex personalities, unaware or scornful of any worries in their daily lives.[7] Her transitional Realism, consequently, can be judged only on the basis of these two cornerstones of her art, which, at the same time, lead to the novel of Regionalism, of local color or *Costumbrismo*, of a novel steeped in national, provincial descriptions. Fernán Caballero followed closely upon the successes of the *costumbristas,* and it is perhaps no coincidence that the *Los españoles pintados por sí mismos* (*The Spaniards Painted by Themselves*), the culmination of the *costumbrista* effort, coincides with the composition of *The Sea Gull.*[8]

For Fernán Caballero, then, her *novela de costumbres* is based on local color sketches which contribute on many occasions nothing to the deemphasized plot and action, but provide, to a degree, an independent unit. Chapters can be read separately as descriptive essays or even as short stories. For example, in the first part, these chapters are illustrative of the essay: Chapter IV provides a view of the abandoned, crumbling monastery near Villamar, the result of the seizure of ecclesiastical property by the central government to secure funds, and is a detailed, architecturally lavish description of the building; Chapter XIV gives a colorful portrayal of the wedding celebrations after the marriage ceremony of Stein and Marisalada, which could be summarized, for plot purposes, in the first sentence, "The wedding of Stein and the Sea Gull was held in the church in Villamar" (I, 54); and in the second part, Chapter I introduces the reader to the social circles of Sevilla at a reception; Chapter II is an impassioned attack on the brutalizing national sport of the bullfight, a Spanish tradition which Fernán Caballero regrets that foreigners accept and applaud so heartily (and from which her hero, Stein, significantly flees in repugnance); Chapter III traces Stein's wanderings through the streets of Sevilla, which he prefers to the horrors of the nearby bullring; Chapter IV offers a literary discussion of the art of the novel among members of the same group as in Chapter I, and is a major treatise on Fernán Caballero's novelistic ideas; and Chapter V, although interrupted by Marisalada's arrival, is a continuation of the previous chapter, with a reflection of the Sevillian society and additional comments on the form of the novel. In the second part, the *costumbrista* sketches are, in general, centered around the aristocracy of Sevilla, to illustrate at close hand Fernán Caballero's knowledge of these activities from her days as the Marquesa de Arco-Hermoso.

These descriptive essays are also complemented by chapters of narrations or short stories in the first part. Chapter VI employs Scott's technique of interrupting the story when a new character is introduced (as happens with Don Modesto Guerrero in Chapter V) to tell his background, the explanation forming a complete vignette in the shy relationship between the officer of Fort St. Christopher and Mystical Rose; Chapter IX, with the Alerza family, Stein's benefactors, seated around the fireplace during an early winter storm, becomes the scene of one story after another, each with a moral and each representative of the Andalusian folklore; and other chapters contribute examples of the narrative tradition in shorter form, mixed with the dialogue of the characters or contained within the progress of the action. Marisalada, for instance, sings a ballad in Chapter X, and Stein realizes that she is on the road to recovery; but this fact of the story is overshadowed in interest by the *romance* (reproduced by Fernán Caballero from her father's collection, which she praises in a footnote of this chapter) and a commentary on the musical treasures of Andalusian folklore. Aunt María is especially versed in this popular heritage of Andalucía, and her examples are numerous, principally for the benefit of the children, who will maintain in their turn this oral tradition for future generations. Fernán Caballero, in one of her digressions, enlarges on this popular spirit in Spanish literature:

It would be difficult for a person, like a child after butterflies, who collects at random these poetic emanations of the people to answer anyone wishing to analyze them why nightingales and linnets mourned the death of the Redeemer; why the swallow wrenched the thorns from His crown; why rosemary is looked upon with a form of veneration in the belief that the Virgin dried the swaddling clothes of the Child Jesus on a bush of that plant; why or rather how it is known that the alder is a tree of bad omen since Judas hanged himself from one of them; why nothing bad will happen to a house if it is made pleasant with rosemary incense on Christmas Night; why all instruments of the Passion are seen in the flower called appropriately by that name. And in truth there is no answer to such questions. The people neither have them nor seek them. The people have collected those examples like vague sounds of a distant music, without inquiring about their origin or analyzing their authenticity. The "enlightened" and "positivists" may possibly honor with a smile of disdainful compassion the person who is composing these lines. But we shall be satisfied with the hope of finding some sympathy in a mother's heart, under the humble roof of someone who knows little and feels much, or in the mystical retreat of a cloister, when we say that for our part we believe that there have always been and there are for pious and ascetic souls mysterious revelations which the world calls deliriums of overexcited imaginations, and which people of meek and fervent faith regard as special favors of God. (I, 26)

The tone is very emphatic in defense of the intuitive wisdom of the people, the traditional faith of Catholicism, and the unquestioning acceptance of folklore—and superstitions—by the centuries. Fernán Caballero, sensitive always to criticism (especially to adverse reactions to her writings), is likewise a combative voice against the philosophies of the modern age. However, her keen and extensive observations stand out admirably in her records of the myriad examples of Andalusian folklore, and she expresses all these varied thoughts poetically and movingly. She is of course digressive and moralizing, and she intrudes her personality without hesitation in order to give more force and assurance to her words.

This defense of the popular tradition, so constant and fervent, won from Benedetto Croce an enthusiastic reception, and the Italian critic placed Fernán Caballero as the only Spanish writer after the Golden Age who merits attention and a separate study.[9] This sweeping, laudatory judgment of Croce, who also calls her "The Catholic Sand" (an unflattering comparison to the French writer probably for Fernán Caballero), is based on her broad adherence to his belief in popularism as the characteristic of Spanish literature, and in explanation of the limited knowledge of this culture outside Spain. "She was animated by a genuine and serious conviction, she possessed a sound judgment," wrote Croce, "and above all because a fountain of poetry sprang from her heart, which is kept alive and fresh even in the midst of the fervent apostolate exercised indefatigably in the service of her faith as a Catholic of the old Church and as a Spaniard of the old Spain."[10] If Fernán Caballero's ideas and beliefs do not interfere with her art, as Croce eloquently pleads, the point is at least mentioned in concession to the numerous objections to the orthodoxy and traditionalism, so amply illustrated in her works.

V The Poetization of Reality

When Fernán Caballero defined her intentions in a novel as "the poetization of reality," she was endeavoring to portray a picture of nature and life, true and accurate in her observations, devoid of the fantastic, exotic descriptions of the Romantics. However, she was a product of the Romantic ambiance through influences of time, parents, and education so that the pictorial quality of Andalusian scenes reflects these sources. At times, her descriptions resemble paintings, similar to those of her friend, the Duque de Rivas, in his plays and poems; the canvases of the French Romantics, such as Delacroix; and the American examples, Cooper in his vision of the hinterland and the Hudson River school of painters. Her Romanticism in descriptive background, subtly conveying the love of nature and the advantages of the simple, harmonious ways of rural life, contributes to poetic, thoughtful frames for the plot; the effectiveness also depends on Fernán Caballero's desire to express openly, strongly, her ideological point of view.

In Chapter V, Stein's impressions of Villamar and the surrounding area form a Romantic mood, prepared of course by his
own innate sentimentality:

> The end of October had been rainy, and November was appearing
> in her heavy, green cloak of winter.
> Stein was walking one day in front of the monastery from where
> an immense and uniform perspective was revealed: to the right, the
> limitless sea; to the left, the endless pasture land. In the middle,
> level with the horizon, the dark profile of the ruins of Fort St.
> Christopher was outlined, like the image of nothingness amidst the
> immensity. The sea, which the slightest gust did not disturb, was
> gently stirring, lifting effortlessly its waves, gilded by the sun's glare,
> like a queen allowing her golden cloak to flow. The monastery, with
> its large, severe, and angular contours, was in harmony with the
> solemn and monotonous landscape; its mass hid the only open
> point of the horizon in that uniform panorama.
> At that point was the village of Villamar, situated beside a river
> as flowing and turbulent in winter, as poor and stagnant in summer.
> The surrounding areas, well cultivated, presented from a distance
> the look of a chessboard, on whose squares the color green varied
> in a thousand ways; here the yellowish grapevine still covered with
> foliage; there the ashy green of an olive tree, or the emerald green
> of wheat, which the autumn rains had caused to shoot forth; or by
> the dark green of the fig trees; and all this divided by the bluish
> green of the plants by the fences. Some fishing boats were crossing
> along the mouth of the river; at the side of the monastery was seen
> a chapel on a hill; in front rose a large cross in the form of a pyramid
> of whitewashed rubblework; behind was an enclosure covered with
> crosses painted black. This was the cemetery. (I, 16)

The grandeur of nature, overpowering and awesome, seems
eternal while the works of man appear small and some buildings
are in ruins—a Romantic concept, standing out sharply in this
passage. The variations on the color green add depth and observation to the surroundings of Villamar; and the changing yet
reliable seasons contribute the sentiment of hope and faith.
Finally, the religious symbol of the cemetery reminds all, subtly
and surely, that man, like the buildings and the seasons, must
vanish; but the image, also a Romantic favorite, is skillfully
placed at the end without a direct moralizing call to traditional
religion.

Thus, when Fernán Caballero's ideology does not get in the

way of her poetic observations and realistic descriptions, or at
least, when her strongly-held views are kept in check by her
artistry, the individual passages increase the aesthetic values of
The Sea Gull. And the lesson or the author's philosophy need not
be omitted, as they are not in the above illustration; but the
tone should not be proselytizing, and the praise of her faith
needs no aura of triumphancy, which Croce grasped as a
defect of Fernán Caballero, to be effective. For example, Stein,
in his arrival at Villamar after the dog's death, viewed essentially
the same scene described at the beginning of the fifth chapter;
but the first painting, poetic and Romantic, is then flawed by
Fernán Caballero's harsh and bitter attack on the decline of tradition and the victory of the liberal, anticlerical government in
Madrid:

> . . . Stein hastened forward but not without shedding copious tears.
> Thus he arrived at the top of another height from where a magnificent
> sight unfolded before his eyes. The terrain descended very im-
> perceptibly toward the sea which reflected calmly and tranquilly
> the fiery sun at its setting, and it seemed like a field sown with
> diamonds, rubies, and sapphires. Among this profusion of splendors
> the white sails of a ship were distinguished, like a pearl and ap-
> parently fixed upon the waves. The irregular coastline now offered
> a beach of golden sand, which the gentle waves splashed with silvery
> foam; jagged and high cliffs, which seemed to take pleasure in
> resisting the terrible element, resisting the onslaughts with firmness
> against fury. In the distance, and on one of the crags at his left,
> the ruins of a fort, a human work resisting nothing, but served by
> a base of rocks, the work of God, resisting everything. Some pine
> trees lifted their strong dark tips, standing out above the thicket.
> To the right, and on top of a hill, was seen a large building; but he
> could not see precisely if it was a town, a castle with surrounding
> areas, or a monastery. (I, 8-9)

This impassioned, intrusive attack of Fernán Caballero,
however, does not appear immediately, but is gradually attuned
to Stein's mood, a skillful procedure in uniting the character's
dejected spirit with the author's reflections on the decline of the
Church. Stein, the Romantic, is intuitively aware of the connotations of his situation and that of the surroundings:

> Almost exhausted by his last flight and the emotion that had upset
> him recently, he headed toward that place.

Night had fallen when he arrived. The building was a monastery like those which were built in past centuries when faith and enthusiasm reigned: virtues so great, so beautiful, so elevated that, for that very reason, they do not belong to this century of narrow and wretched ideas; because, then, gold did not serve to be hoarded nor to be used for luxuries but was given for worthy and noble uses inasmuch as men thought of the grand and beautiful. It was a monastery that, in other sumptuous times, being rich and hospitable, gave bread to the poor, help to the wretched, and cured the ills of soul and body; but now, abandoned, empty, poor, dilapidated, placed on sale for some pieces of paper, no one had wanted to buy it, not even at such a low price.

Speculation, though grown to gigantic dimensions, though advancing like a conqueror invading everything, not shrinking from obstacles, usually stops nevertheless in front of the dwelling places of the Lord, like the sand carried away by the desert wind stops at the foot of the Pyramids. (I, 9)

Fortunately, Fernán Caballero seldom loses her talent to employ poetical imagery, even in defense of this attack on the confiscation of church lands, between 1836 and 1844, by the government as revenge for clerical aid to the Carlists, a general anticlerical policy and to secure funds quickly. In this idealized, romanticized version of the medieval and Golden Age past, when men lived for the glories of the Church and worked for their fellows (the concept of the Golden Age with humanity living in harmony is, of course, an important belief of Don Quijote in his speech to the goatherds), Fernán Caballero demonstrates her Romanticism and fails to keep a realistic, historical, accurate gauge of those less than perfect times. At the same time, curiously, she shows herself cognizant and prophetic about the nascent problems of the nineteenth century: the transformation of society as a result of money being the center of interest and power. She probed in *Lágrimas* vaguely and with her mind set against the changing values to such an extent that she refused to analyze the contemporary issues, the consequences for Villamar of the nineteenth century. Her timid approaches, however, are very valuable: she opened the door (for a horrified peek) at precisely the perplexities of the age which Galdós treated to become the Balzac, one of Fernán Caballero's idols, of the modern Spanish novel. And, indeed, Galdós objected to Fernán Caballero's novelistic achievements on the grounds that she had concentrated on her Andalusian sketches instead of dealing with the urban middle class where is occurring "the marvelous drama of present-day life."[11] Nevertheless, as Montesinos repeatedly insists in his "essay of justification," Fernán Caballero, by dint of getting her feet wet in the turbulent, unpleasant waters of the contemporary age and by calling attention—critically prejudiced and constantly opposed—to the transitional years she was observing, rendered a singular service to the modern novel.

There is no accidental, theoretical venture in these conclusions because Fernán Caballero was deliberately endeavoring to immerse herself, without abandoning her faith in the past, in the world of this unacceptable nineteenth century. "I am writing now, still in French, a novel to describe the present state of society," Fernán Caballero explained in a letter about *The Sea Gull*, "the epoch of transition in which the old is driven out by something new, still immature."[12] If Villamar in 1848 is being transformed, then the roots of these alterations were planted earlier, in 1838, when Stein meditated upon the ruinous effects of the seizures and neglect of ecclesiastical properties and the decline of the chivalric ideals of service to the Church. Fernán Caballero, in her determination to defend the past and national traditions, emphasized repeatedly and poignantly her interpretation of the truth, under the Romantic aegis, of the "poetization of reality." Later, after the success of *The Sea Gull*, she wrote in another letter: "Upon poetizing the truth, which is my whole concern and my high aim, I fear that this truth I love may not appear in all its splendor."[13] Truth, then, at the base of her artistic construction, is a personal, poetical interpretation of a philosophy; and the effort to separate the realistic, local color sketches of impeccable observations from the Romantic, ideological aspects is exacted of the objective reader.

VI   *The World Outside*

This problem of the truth and poetry in *The Sea Gull* diminishes in the second part when the action is transferred to the cities of Sevilla and Madrid. There is really only one episode reminiscent of the idealized, *costumbrista* life of Villamar, and this third chapter is brief, objective, and historical—Stein's escape from the bullfight to view the sights of Sevilla. This vignette is also the singular, favorable, and detailed account of the two cities which, for the duration of the second part, only exist in the salons and homes of the characters, major and minor. The planned absence of any descriptions perhaps indicates Fernán Caballero's disregard of whatever might be pleasant in the urban centers.

However, Fernán Caballero can contribute a very precise and accurate rendition of the Spanish institution she detests thoroughly, the bullfight. The second chapter, important for the plot because Marisalada and Pepe Vera see each other for the first time, provides a vehement attack on the performance, the appeal, morbid and sadistic, for natives and foreigners, and the abhorrence of crowds, noise, and vulgarity:

> When Stein and María arrived at the bullring in the afternoon, it was already full of people. A sustained and animated noise served as a prelude to the performance like rough and roaring waves before the storm. That immense gathering, to which the whole population of the city and its environs comes; that agitation similar to that of the blood pounding in the heart in the frenzy of a violent passion; that ardent, intoxicating atmosphere like that surrounding a drunken, riotous woman; that function of innumerable feelings into a single one; that feverish expectation; that frenetic exaltation, repressed, nevertheless, within the limits of order; those noisy shouts, but without any coarseness; that impatience which fear serves as a tonic; that anxiety which communicates shivers of pleasure—form a kind of electric shock to which it is necessary to yield or to flee. (I, 74)

The impression, subtle but sure, is conveyed that the vice of this national sport brings out the worst elements in the urban populace and in human nature generally. The bullfight is unfortunately a Spanish attraction for foreigners, providing them with the incorrect picture of Spain, as Fernán Caballero lamented in the prologue to *The Sea Gull*, so that "bullfights delight foreigners of depraved taste or who are surfeited with all the pleasures of life, and who long for a thrill, for a shock (like cold water) to revive them; or they delight the mass of Spaniards, energetic and unsentimental, and who, moreover, have been accustomed since childhood to this kind of spectacle," and "on the other hand, many attend out of habit; others, especially women, to see and to be seen; others who go to the bullfights suffer and are not amused, but they remain, thanks to the part of our human nature which makes us like sheep and with which we are liberally endowed" (I, 75).

The bullfights, of course, are generally but not necessarily familiar in the cities instead of the countryside; and Fernán Caballero, very clearly, has profited by this opportunity to attack two opponents of true Spanish ways and life. More directly, she can criticize a phenomenon of the cities, newspapers, by commenting acidly in the chapter on the bullfight that "we offer sincere congratulations to the newspapers which have taken the initiative in the Spanish press against the unheard-of cruelty with which the poor animals are treated here, and which have asked that the agony of the wretched animals be ended by a knife thrust," but "as freedom of the press is of no service to good causes (which it might serve), such just and charitable advice has not been paid any attention."[14] Momo's humorous report to Villamar after his futile mission to have Marisalada return to see her dying father is replete with snide references to the discourteous behavior and the drunken habits of the city dwellers. Momo, of course, is the victim of his own ignorance about life outside Villamar; and his adventures are ironical, considering his sharp tongue. But Fernán Caballero, nonetheless, employs a subtle yet convincing technique to persuade her audience that there are few advantages in the cities among strangers.

However, the principal urban dwellers encountered in the second part are aristocrats and members of wealthy families, and here is the occasion for Fernán Caballero to criticize most harshly the modes of high society. The characters in the salons of Sevilla and Madrid are illustrative of the four types of Spaniards outlined by the author in the prologue to *The Sea Gull*, and the arguments provide endless debating points for all these opposing points of view. Probably interesting for contemporary readers of *The Sea Gull*, since these representatives of high society have been mentioned as some evidence that the novel is a *roman à clef*, based solidly on the author's observations as the Marquesa de Arco-Hermoso, the commentaries have undoubtedly less relevance for present-day audiences.[15] And, in fact, Ochoa fully grasped this possibility at that time and preferred the first part.[16] The contrast is clear between the local color sketches and stories of the chapters in Villamar, which still retain interest as well as historical value, and the polished, frivolous, and often hypocritical chatter of the drawing rooms. The action is halted, the motivation is lacking for audience reaction, no artistic revelations come forth; and, in short, these lengthy scenes represent the weakest element in the construction of *The Sea Gull.* The unimportance of high society, which may have been one of Fernán Caballero's aims, is lost in an unsuccessful literary treatment, remedied easily by the simple omission of so many pages of tedious conversations.

VII   *What Is A Novel?*

The redeeming feature, however, of the dialogues in the salons during the second part—and the valuable contribution for an understanding of *The Sea Gull* as a novel, the author's theories, and the novelistic art—is the debate about the Spanish novel. The discussions should, of course, reflect the viewpoints outlined in the prologue, and they do confirm and amplify that brief theory of the Realistic novel, or the "antinovel," as Montesinos theorizes.[17]

Rafael, perhaps the liveliest and most sympathetic guest at the various gatherings in the second part, proposes that all contribute to the composition of a novel; and the argument erupts immediately and with animated disagreement about the question: What is a novel? If the novel is written in French, published serially, and with seductions and adulteries, then it will be an imitation of the prevailing currents and nothing original. "It's not a good idea to make women interesting because of their faults," and "nothing is less interesting in the eyes of sensible people than to see a light-headed girl letting herself be seduced, or a lewd woman cheating on her husband," declares the Countess of Algar's mother, the Marchioness; and this perhaps expresses a literary presentation of the views (and differences) between Doña Cecilia and Doña Frasquita before 1838. Ironically, of course, the three characteristics of the novel at that time, noted above, refer to *The Sea Gull.*

Suicide is banished from the novel, "frightful suicide, unknown here until now, and which has succeeded in weakening if not in destroying the Faith" (I, 83), a dictum which Fernán Caballero obeyed in all her stories, but certainly a tragic statement in view of Arrom de Ayala's later suicide. The pithy definition of Fernán Caballero's *novela de costumbres* is then stated, appropriately by the Countess of Algar: "We are not to paint the Spanish people as foreigners; we shall portray ourselves as we are" (I, 83). Stein prophetically asks: "But with the restrictions imposed by the Marchioness, what kind of romantic outcome can a novel have which is generally based on an unfortunate passion?" (I, 83). The clue to the final chapter of *The Sea Gull*, after the letter explaining Stein's romantic fate, is then given as "Time makes an end to all, no matter what the novelists say who dream instead of observing; besides, can't there be any other theme but an unfortunate passion?" (I, 83-84).

The new novel should have no ostentation in the form of foreign words and phrases, but, instead, the language should be rooted firmly in the dictionary—accepted usage of the Spanish language, as defined by the Royal Spanish Academy. Euphuisms are to be avoided; "God" is preferable to the high-sounding expressions of the Enlightenment, these in order to avoid the question of a direct, firm faith. Fernán Caballero's worthwhile defense of simplicity of language is shrewdly blended with her advocacy of traditional, orthodox religious values. This imaginary exercise in the composition of a novel deals with the issue of the subjects, and the Countess suggests that "let us put aside any weaknesses, tears, crimes, and exaggerated expressions," and "let us make something good, elegant and cheerful" (I, 84). However, Rafael objects that virtue, or pure goodness, throughout a novel would result in an insipid, flat story; and, in short, that the warp and woof of the novel is the deviation from the path of noble and normal behavior.

How should this new novel be classified as to genre? Stein, reflecting his German background (as Rafael in opposition suggests), proposes "a fantastic novel," which is rejected on the complaint that "a Spanish fantastic novel would be an unbearable affectation" (I, 84). This Gothic novel is then balanced by Stein with the other type of Romantic novel, the heroic, sad, or sentimental story; but Rafael finally ends any attempt to impose a current, Romantic mode: "There is no type which is less suited to the Spanish temper than the weeping type" (I, 84). A division of the novelistic art is proposed as "the historical novel, which we shall leave to learned writers, and the novel of customs, which is exactly the right one for mediocre writers like us" (I, 85); and the Countess, accepting immediately this promising solution, is rewarded by Rafael with this advocacy of the new novel, the *novela de costumbres*:

> It is the very best novel . . . useful and agreeable. Each nation should write its own. Written with accuracy and with a true spirit of observation, they would help a great deal in the study of humanity, history, moral practice, and for the knowledge of times and places. If I were the queen, I would order a novel of customs to be written in every province, without omitting anything in references and analyses. (I, 85)

This discussion is dominated by Rafael throughout the remainder of this chapter. Humorously and without any malice, he sets himself up as the new novelist of the *novela de costumbres* by offering his uncle, General Santa María, as the subject for the book "because if Madame de Staël has said that the life of a woman is always a novel, I think that, with equal right, one may say that the life of a man is always a history" (I, 85). Although the whole narration of the general's life, personality, and antecedents is conducted without any anger resulting from the explanations, nevertheless the literary problem forms a subtle, important undercurrent: how should a novel of customs adhere to the line of accuracy? Rafael is in favor of including the less appealing traits of his uncle and downgrading the unverified traditions of the general's family and ancestors; the Marchioness restrains Rafael (with verbal opposition rather than with convincing proof) in his efforts to demolish myths in favor of truth by preferring to maintain the pleasant traditions and felicitous memories of the past. Fernán Caballero's effort at the "poetization of reality," which for her is the truth of Andalusian local color sketches, a combination of Realism and Romanticism, can be perceived in the friendly exchanges between Rafael and the Marchioness, conducted with all the civilities in the novels of Jane Austen.

Later, but very briefly, the conversations at one of the many social gatherings in the second part treat of the problems of the modern novel; and the references, slight and oblique, bring the author into the scope of the artistic creation. The Countess of Algar (or perhaps Fernán Caballero), when presented a copy of

Dumas' *Voyage Through the South of France,* comments that an author is rendered disservice when the applause and flattery are inane or given by foolish admirers, lacking any real comprehension of the writer's work. Criticism, of course, is the right of the public about any artist who offers himself as the target when he publishes a book, a surprising comment by Fernán Caballero in light of her future sensitivity to adverse reactions about her writings. A very personal explanation about her wish for anonymity (and the use of a pen name, indirectly) as well as the desire to be a writer supplies a sound basis for the issue of the two individuals, the woman and the author:

"In general, knowing writers of great merit has inconvenient aspects."

"Why, Countess?"

"Because the usual result is that this personal knowledge is disparaging to the author. A friend of mine, a person of much talent, used to say that great men are the opposite of statues because the latter seem larger and the former smaller as one draws near to them. As for me, if sometime I become an author (which may possibly happen, if it is true that all of us have a bit of the poet and the madman), at least I will have the advantage that I am heard without being seen, thanks to my smallness, the slight brilliance of my pen, and distance."

"Do you then believe that the author should be one of the heroes of his fiction?"

"No, but I should fear to see him giving the lie to the ideas and sentiments that he expresses, and then the spell would be broken because, upon reading what he had taken away from me, I would not be able to get rid of the idea that the man had written it with his head and not with his heart." (I, 93-94)

In short, Fernán Caballero, by 1845, during the writing of *The Sea Gull,* had evolved a theory of the modern novel and the role of the novelist, not necessarily intrusive, but certainly faithful to feelings and observations. Her terminology may be awkward, such as the classifications of the historical novel and the novel of customs; but her general understanding of the new novel, where, in the prologue to *The Sea Gull,* the same unsure manner of defining the two strands of the nineteenth-century novel is also apparent, is clear and sound: the Romantic novel is unsatisfactory in a rapidly changing age and is unsuited for a faithful portrait of Spain (and any other country in this period), and a new novel, rooted in observation and local color sketches, is the answer for the revival of the novelistic genre.

VIII   *The Physiology of Characterization*

Rafael, as a compliment to Stein during the important discussion about the novel at the Countess of Algar's home, remarks that "Don Federico, since you are an observant physiologist, you must admire how, in all the situations of life in Spain, evenness of temper, benevolence, and even joy, are unchangeable. We do not have here the melancholy of the Germans, the spleen of the English, or the boredom of our neighbors, the French. Do you know why? Because we do not demand too much of life, because we do not pant after cheap success" (I, 82). Fernán Caballero's frequent praises of Balzac and her predilection for quotations from the French novelist also extended to her mutual interest in "physiologies," which, as Montesinos has consistently proved,[18] was transferred to the generic, abstract plane in characterization. She, therefore, withdrew from the Balzacian concern about pathological, disparate personages; and she converted her characters into class representatives, adding at times her philosophical, ideological views to the portraits. "When Fernán does not sketch her characters with hostile aims for anyone," concludes Montesinos, "when she forgets her social and literary preoccupations and obtains objectivity which she lacks so many times, she succeeds in bringing about an indulgent tolerance which the famous 'sermonizing' especially emphasizes. She noted it, yet without comprehending perhaps the cause. All that part of her work is that which, historically at least, continues to have a high value."[19]

Therefore, characterization has received recognition from critics, beginning again with Ochoa who also preferred the residents of Villamar to the society of Sevilla and Madrid, although he gave credit for the verisimilitude of the latter personages. Most of the characters in *The Sea Gull*, then, in accord with Montesinos' analysis, do not emerge as individuals, but rather as types so that characterization, in all fairness, is not a major contribution of Fernán Caballero to the Realistic novel. The minor characters, divided sharply into rural and urban types, can be swiftly noted by one function, role, or ideal. In the first part, Aunt María is the conservative, traditionalist, and orthodox peasant woman, perhaps the epitome of Fernán Caballero's longing for the Spain of the past (whatever that might be); and Aunt María is also the maternal image, intervening in almost all matters inside and outside the home. This is a far cry from García Lorca's twentieth-century vision in *La casa de Bernarda Alba* (*The House of Bernarda Alba*). Brother Gabriel, the victim of anticlericalism and the decline of the Church's power, symbolizes the highest aspirations of the religious ideal (representatives of the clergy are consistently portrayed flatteringly in Fernán Caballero's stories) and is a model of goodness, placidity, and generosity. He, like Aunt María, cannot really exist in the Villamar of 1848, and it is no accident that their deaths are reported in the last chapter of *The Sea Gull*. The members of the Alerza family, Manuel and Dolores, together with their children (except Momo), appear little in the novel, have minor parts; but they are likewise indicative of the respectful, dutiful, hard-working peasants encountered often in the *comedias* (dramas) of the Golden Age, especially in those of Lope de Vega. Don Modesto Guerrero, like Brother Gabriel, is the declining symbol of another pillar of the Spanish past, the military power; and this officer of the equally aging fort is an example of the noble, brave, and self-sacrificing soldier, who is also an anachronism, even at the novel's beginning. Mystical Rose, the schoolmistress and shy housekeeper for Don Modesto Guerrero (their comical, platonic, and somewhat pathetic relationship is sketched winningly in the sixth chapter), is a prim and proper guardian of the town's youngsters, and is very perceptive about Marisalada's unpleasant nature, after a few adventures in the classroom. Ramón Pérez, the barber's son, plays the less than heroic part of the local Don Juan, a prototype of other sundry characters in Fernán Caballero's works, never favored as exemplary by the writer.

Two minor characters of Villamar do not follow so rigidly this pattern of types: Pedro Santaló and Momo. The fisherman, one of the most appealing and realistic characters in the novel, is based possibly on Balzac's Goriot;[20] or, at the very least, Marisalada's father undergoes the same torments of ingratitude and suffering as Old Goriot. Santaló is not the Romantic hero, as

Stein shows so clearly; but is instead, for Fernán Caballero, the true image of fatherhood, especially the Spanish father, just as his counterpart, Aunt María, is the Spanish mother. Momo is the best-sketched character in *The Sea Gull;* he is a well-rounded personality, despite his antipathetic role. Momo owes the most to Fernán Caballero's interest in physiology, that popular science of her formative years, in that he does not fit conveniently, as do the others above indicated, into the rigid mold of a type, expressive of a trait in the author's vision of a traditionalist Spain. In addition, Momo is reminiscent of a native influence from Spanish literature, the *gracioso,* or comic foil from the Golden Age *comedia.* Momo is unpleasant, ungenerous, undisciplined; he is a picaresque figure and is certainly an anti-hero, whom no one wants to imitate. However, his place in the novel, structurally, as an independent character, and as the spokesman for Fernán Caballero, is unquestioned. Without Momo, much of the humor, coarse and brutally frank, would be lost in the novel; and the Romantic plot, headed by the sympathetic Stein, would be in the pure vein of sentimentalism. Momo's interventions in the first part bring not only comic relief to the serious commentaries and compelling reactions of Stein to his new environment; the remarks of Momo contribute a realistic—and different—tone to the *costumbrista* impressions, so dominant and repetitive. In short, Momo is the only character of Villamar who is not idealized and stereotyped; he is not good, kind, and soft-spoken. The irony and the literary success of Fernán Caballero reside in her rendition of Momo as the only person (with the occasional comments of Mystical Rose) who sees Marisalada truthfully.

Momo, from his first encounter with Stein and Marisalada, warned everyone that, by taking charge of the girl, "you'll go to a lot of trouble with that crow who'll pick out your eyes . . . you'll see how you'll get paid back, sooner or later" (I, 32). Momo's voice is the warning signal, even during the wedding day when he takes a reluctant part in the festivities, that Marisalada is still a "Sea Gull." Momo illustrates the problem of personality in his naturally belligerent, ill-natured ways; and Aunt María, attempting to have Momo volunteer for the trip to Madrid when Pedro Santaló is fatally ill, wonders aloud about the explanation for her grandson's miserable behavior. No other member of her family, she sadly ponders, is so uncharitable; and no one, certainly, takes out his frustrations on the animals of the vicinity. Some explanation, of course, is found in Momo's physical appearance: he is ugly as Fernán Caballero graphically describes him at his first appearance in the novel: "At this moment Momo appeared at the kitchen door. He was short and chubby, with high shoulders, which he had the bad habit of holding even higher, in a scornful gesture of 'What do I care,' until they touched his big ears, stretching out like fans. He had a large head, short hair, thick lips; and in addition, was flat-nosed and horribly cross-eyed" (I, 10-11). Momo, unlike Quasimodo in Hugo's *The Hunchback of Notre Dame*, is no Romantic figure, ugly in body and noble in heart; but, instead, Momo is a Realistic character, despite this accidental (or perhaps imitative) resemblance to the cathedral bellringer. His peasant wit and native intelligence, like Sancho Panza's, are compounded with proverbs and moral sayings, which belie his lack of education and apparent stupidity.

Fernán Caballero, of course, does not probe the complexities of Momo; and she omits any investigation of her character's vile temper and disagreeable behavior, unlike the Balzacian mastery of physiology. Momo, instead of a profound character study, is converted into the literary expression of Fernán Caballero's verdict on Marisalada. The brilliance of this artistic performance is the omission thereby of direct intervention by the writer in overt moralizing and didactic insertions; and the fact that Momo, an ugly, unappealing character, is employed for this artistic aim is a strong point in favor of Fernán Caballero's ˙novelistic maturity. Incomparably effective (and devastating for the humbled "Sea Gull") is the remembrance of things past, all bad, that Momo shouts with glee at Marisalada in the last chapter. She can never escape Momo's cruel, truthful sermons about her misdeeds and failures, especially in the small area of Villamar; and where all the inhabitants look scornfully at her. And, perhaps, Momo's success—and convenience for the novelist—are demonstrated in Fernán Caballero's use of Momo again, in the continuation of Villamar's history in *Lágrimas*.

The personages in the city radiate no varieties of characterization, falling within the ideological divisions of Spaniards, outlined in the prologue; or they adhere to the author's idealized portraits, such as the Duke and Duchess of Almansa and the Sister of Charity. Even Pepe Vera is a stereotype, a mixture of Don Juan and *machismo*, or supposedly Spanish manliness; and his counterpart is the village Lothario, Ramón Pérez—comically called by Momo as Ratón (Rat) instead of "Ramón." The participants at the *tertulias*, however, are not unpleasant personalities; but the nature of the social gatherings, governed by rigid rules of conduct, prevents any person from veering significantly from the expected norms of conversation. Some guests, in fact, offer charming aspects of their personalities, such as Rafael; but the explanation for the generally bland portraits is that Fernán Caballero preferred the villagers as examples for the *novela de costumbres*. The very pronounced division of her characters into peasant, rural types, and aristocratic, urban representatives is the work of her belief in this traditional class structure. Her failure to include any members of the *bourgeoisie* lacks thereby an important Realistic trait in the novel, grasped brilliantly by her idol, Balzac, and developed extensively by her successor, Galdós. In *Lágrimas*, unfortunately a less popular but more contemporary novel than *The Sea Gull*, the recognition of the middle-class arrival upon the Spanish scene provides an insight into actual conditions, realistically and prophetically.

The two main characters, Stein and Marisalada, reverse the importance of their roles in the two parts: the first part is the story of Stein, who dominates completely this division, but loses this importance at the moment of decision to leave Villamar; the second part revolves about the experiences of Marisalada, and Stein has few appearances, finally leaving Spain, and whose death is related by Rafael through a farewell letter. Stein, though praised by Ochoa as a noble, correct, and romantic soul, stands out as, quite simply, too perfect; his frequent tears are the signs of an extravagant Romanticism, and the author has endowed Stein with all the birthmarks of a true Romantic. He is German, a lover of music and nature, melancholy, sentimental, and idealistic; he is a spiritual heir of Goethe's creations, and in the very first chapter of *The Sea Gull*, Stein is sarcastically called by one of the anonymous passengers on the ship, a "weepy Werther" (I, 6). Stein, in brief, is almost a caricature of the early Romantic hero, although Fernán Caballero probably did not intend to evoke such a reaction.

On the other hand, Marisalada is the first in the series of memorable feminine characters created by Fernán Caballero. Ochoa realized the artistry and forceful characterization of Fernán Caballero's portrait in this wide-ranging analysis:

But the figure who brings irresistibly greatest interest to the reader, the one who always dominates the scene, because she is never indifferent for us if certainly she is almost always antipathetic, is the character of Marisalada. Nothing more singular, nothing more illogical, and for that very reason perhaps, nothing more interesting than that sullen character, cold and passionate at the same time, ferociously hard and capable, nevertheless, in love of the most abject servility; a woman fanciful like a fairy at times, and at other times, prosaic and groveling like a little girl; an inexplicable combination but which is felt and seen, and in which one believes as in a living thing, of sensitivity and indifference, of beauty and physical and moral ugliness, of goodness and depravity, both innate, of sublime talent and gross materialism, a character whom it is impossible to love and nevertheless whom we do not find it easy to hate; a character highly complex who, on the one hand, is close to the uncultured simplicity of savage nature and, on the other hand, indulges in the impurest refinements of social corruption. There are in Marisalada something of the indolent and malign condition of Cooper's Indian and something also of George Sand's free woman. If the author has copied from life that very singular personage, she is a skillful and sagacious observer; if she has taken her from her imagination, she is a great poet; at any rate, she is a profound connoisseur of the human heart. That is why, without doubt, she does not insist upon explaining the motive of her protagonist's actions. To what end? Not even the most ingenious explanation could seem satisfactory for those who know that there is nothing in the world more irrational than passion as there is nothing, many times, more improbable than truth itself. "The Sea Gull" is a character purely of passion; reason has no dominion over her. The same, somewhat foolish spontaneity, the same, somewhat brutal obstinacy that we find in her first words when the author introduces her on stage, we see in all her acts until the end of the novel. (V, 434-35)

Ochoa, of course, is less harsh on Marisalada than Fernán Caballero, both within the novel and within other writings about wayward women, would seem to indicate; and the Spanish critic even objected in his review that the incident of the love affair between Marisalada and Pepe Vera has debased cruelly the girl's character. However, Fernán Caballero does attempt, too briefly and too sketchily, to analyze Marisalada's personality; and the results are an important advance in the direction of characterization, or physiologies if the Balzacian interest is pursued. In fairness to Marisalada, the first fact is that, quite simply, she was never in love with Stein and, indeed, she did not want to get married. If one probes deeper the girl's complex personality, the second fact emerges that she, for unexplained reasons, resented her father and eagerly looked for the opportunity to leave the fisherman's humble home. She is of course arrogant at this point, before entering a higher level of society; and her misplaced pride may be some rationalization. Another more tantalizing issue arises in her insistence, when Stein wants to kiss her after their agreement to marry, " 'Not that!' said María, stepping back rapidly and frowning, 'no one touches me!' " (I, 52). There is also an indication within the later chapters that Stein and Marisalada occupied separate bedrooms; and the possibility arises as an answer to some of Marisalada's heartless treatments and remarks that the marriage was never consummated, although Fernán Caballero, of course, fails to hint more overtly at a more advanced psychological argument. These themes in literature will have to await the Naturalists, such as Clarín in *La Regenta* (*The Regent's Wife*), Emilia Pardo Bazán (perhaps the feminine successor to Fernán Caballero as a novelist in the second half of the nineteenth century), and Blasco Ibáñez.

Conversely, Marisalada shows the other side of her personality, the passionate, irrational side, as Ochoa indicated, when she falls instantly in love with Pepe Vera at the bullfight (and the latter, as Fernán Caballero stresses, corresponds wholeheartedly):

> The duke fixed his attention on Marisalada. It was the first time since her arrival in the capital of Andalucía that he noted some emotion on that cold and disdainful face. Until that moment he had never seen her animated. María's rough appearance, too vulgar to surrender to the exquisite sentiment of admiration and too indifferent and cold to surrender to surprise, had not deigned to admire anything nor to show any interest. It was necessary to make use of fire and hammer to make an impression, to get some spark from that hard metal. (I, 76)

Marisalada, once in the throes of passion (a mysterious force for many of Fernán Caballero's female characters), commits herself totally, needs a corresponding partner, and comes alive as a woman, thus offering a brilliantly contemporary theme in literature, unhappily depicted only in glimpses in *The Sea Gull;* as, for example, in this scene between Marisalada and Pepe Vera:

> Those coarse and brutal lovers seemed more like tigers than human beings. And that is the way that modern literature usually depicts distinguished gentlemen and elegant ladies!
>
> In that brief moment, those two natures sounded out each other, mutually, and they knew that they were of the same temper and strength. It was necessary to cut off their relations or to stop fighting. Each one gave up the victory, because of a reciprocal instinct of this. (I, 177)

Finally, at the bullfight where Pepe Vera has brutally forced Marisalada to attend from fear of losing him, she is torn between her resentment at having been roused from her sickbed and her undeniable, overpowering love:

> She leaned against the railing and she had pressed her fingernails into it, for she loved that young and handsome man whom she saw so serene while facing death. She was pleased by a love that subjugated her, that made her tremble, that brought tears to her; because that brutal and tyrannical love, on the other hand, was profound, passionate, and exclusive, and it was love she needed, as certain men of a rough nature need whiskey to get drunk, and not sweet liqueurs and light wines. (I, 127)

Marisalada, understood in the light of a passionate woman requiring a strong mate, stands out as a memorable feminine character, despite objectionable manners and verbal rudeness in Villamar and the cities. Fernán Caballero has also sketched a vivid, lifelike model for her other novels and stories; but she has more importantly contributed the portrait of the nineteenth-century woman for literature, independent, strong-willed, and in defiance of social canons, despite the moralizing, sermonizing victory of her creator, deserving obviously and certainly an equitable punishment.

IX *The Lady Preacher*

No critic, sympathetic or unfavorable to Fernán Caballero's effort in *The Sea Gull* (and other works), denies that the personal, intrusive ideas and beliefs of the author lack an objective, positive quality in the novel when these views become a repeated, dogmatic aspect of this artistic creation. Of course, every literary work reflects the writer's philosophy, and a novelist is certainly within his domain to insert these ideological orientations—if the book in question is not converted into a proselytizing tract. There seems critically no disagreement that Fernán Caballero's defect in *The Sea Gull* is her undue emphasis upon her faith in the traditional values of Spain.[21]

The Church is the mainstay, for Fernán Caballero, of a virtuous, individual morality and the source of charitable, chivalric ideals; and the physical features of Catholic power in Villamar and Sevilla add beauty, inspiration, and a sense of history to the landscape and for the benefit of the people. The neglect of the ecclesiastical properties provides a springboard for an attack on the Enlightenment and Liberalism as the causes for this decline of the Church. Fernán Caballero's simplistic interpretation of history revolves around the failure to remain in place: every motion forward since 1700 (when the Bourbons from France ascended the Spanish throne and brought with them foreign models) has really been a step backward. In the last chapter of *The Sea Gull*, "the novelties of the time" brought the use of contemporary, political names for roads, etc., instead of saints' names as in the past; and Mystical Rose suspiciously comments upon the Pope's mildly liberal reforms. In 1848, Pius IX had of course acquired the reputation since his election two years previously of a pontiff of the nineteenth century, unlike his immediate predecessors in Rome. Symbolically perhaps, Brother Gabriel's death, reported in the last paragraph of *The Sea Gull*, reads like the continuing decline of Catholicism, a decline accelerated by the seizure of Church lands in the 1830's which Fernán Caballero—and her characters, Stein, Aunt María, and others—strongly criticized in the novel's first part. These fears, pessimism, and sadness coincide with the appearance of the Catholic traditionalists, Jaime Balmes and Juan Donoso Cortés, who in their writings espoused similar attitudes.[22]

Santaló's death provides Fernán Caballero with the occasion for her most vehement defense of Catholicism. The scene, Romantic, melodramatic, and compellingly effective as a climactic moment of the plot, is marred by the scar of Catholic triumphalism.

"Nothing could give splendor and life to this moral truth, as the way we have just described it," insists Fernán Caballero, "that in the midst of the tumult and tempests of evil passions, the voice of holy religion allows itself to be heard at intervals, grave and powerful, soft and firm even to those very ones who forget and deny it" (I, 115). Indeed, Fernán Caballero, in these sincere, fervent, but artistically weak sermons, resembles a preacher more than a convincing novelist: "Catholics maintain for death all the solemn respect that God has given it by His adoption of it as a sacrifice in expiation.... All was repose and peace inside because God despoils death of its horrors and anxieties when the soul is raised to heaven with the cry for mercy, being surrounded by fervent hearts on earth repeating: mercy, mercy!" (I, 115).

The aristocracy and, concomitantly, the monarchy (although this institution is seldom mentioned in *The Sea Gull*), serve as the model and guide of good manners, moral leadership, and maintenance of political stability in Fernán Caballero's Spain; and the Duke of Almansa, from his introduction in the first chapter, always behaves as an exemplary nobleman, despite his vague infatuation for Marisalada, which he humbly confesses to the duchess, an equivalent portrait of the noblewoman. All the participants at the social gatherings in Sevilla and Madrid are, as members of the ruling class, directed by patriotic, national sentiments toward Spain—a spiritual pride in the homeland, closely associated with aristocratic and humble characters alike. There are differences of opinion about love of country and the defense of Spanish ways of life, but Fernán Caballero ardently espouses the cause of Spain. She is also optimistic about the values of the country, and the advantages far outweigh any vices, such as the bullfight.

Fernán Caballero is, then, essentially conservative, conformist, and traditionalist; and she dreads, for example, the word "progress" as a code term for the worst of possible worlds, a "progress" which is advancing for the erosion of the above-mentioned institutions, already in sad disarray. The world of Fernán Caballero may be summarized by the dates of *The Sea Gull*: in 1848, when the novel ends, the internal changes, the European revolutions, and even papal liberalism, have converted Villamar (and Spain) into a tragic caricature of the village of 1838, when Stein arrived in the second chapter, and where the old life is being swept away by the outside whirlwinds of change. If Fernán Caballero could have stopped at the present, at 1838, she would not have been overjoyed at this theoretical compromise because, in short, even the many local color sketches, extensively and lovingly described in the book's first part, would not have signified the realization of her ideology. For the impossible vision of Fernán Caballero, for her "exact, true, and genuine idea of Spain," as she declares in *The Sea Gull's* prologue, ten years earlier—1828—characterized the ideal period when Spanish traditions and institutions held unchallenged sway over the national life and governance.

The observations, descriptions, and folklore of Andalucía—Fernán Caballero's art at its best in *The Sea Gull*—and the scenes, also, in Sevilla and Madrid emerge, not as the literary rendition of foreign influences and readings (although these aspects are not completely discounted), but as the author's interests and experiences as the Marquesa de Arco-Hermoso in the Andalusian village of Dos Hermanas, other picturesque vicinities, and the two cities mentioned above. Fernán Caballero recalled her own days, the happiest of her life, as she once admitted, and referred in *The Sea Gull* to this better world (a decade before the novel's beginning) when the future for her seemed destined to be a continuation of the present. This vision, of course, corresponded only in part to the historical, political realities of the reign of Fernando VII; but the personal promise around this year, 1828, when she met Washington Irving and was occupied in "compiling and copying" (as she defined the *novela de costumbres*) coincided with a felicitous if illusory ideology about Spain and Spanish life. Her backward rather than forward view, nevertheless, won audiences at that time and literary immortality, with autobiographical, impressionistic strands woven skillfully in a *costumbrista*, realistic, and photographic embroidery.

CHAPTER 3

A Story of Rural Life

L A FAMILIA DE ALVAREDA (*The Family of Alvareda*), published
first as *La familia Alvareda* in *El Heraldo* from September
7th until September 26, 1849, provided Fernán Caballero with
her second outstanding success of that year; and the novel has
been documented and traced to greater extent than any of her
other books, with the result that the first draft can be assigned
a rather firm date of 1828 and the final form in the complete
works of 1856.[1] The story, if not the earliest literary attempt of
Doña Cecilia, is certainly the first significant novel she wrote;
and *The Family of Alvareda* is often favored as her more permanent contribution to Spanish literature, although *The Sea
Gull*, of course, retains stature as the first published novel of
Fernán Caballero.[2] But it is impossible and unfair to grant
somewhat arbitrarily the classification of "best" novel to either
of the two. *The Family of Alvareda* has undoubtedly received
a very favorable recognition outside Spain in translations, and
in texts for secondary schools and higher education in the
United States.[3]

I *A Tale of Sex and Violence*

Fernán Caballero, in "a word to the reader" to introduce her
"original novel of popular customs," explains that:

The plot of this novel, which we have announced as destined
exclusively to paint the people, is a real fact, and the narration,
faithful in the main, to the point of having kept the same expressions
used by those who figure in it, without doing any more than omitting
occasionally some crudeness. Also, the action has been transferred
to a period prior to the one in which it took place, and something
has been added at the beginning and at the end.

We are not unaware that, with the elements lent by the case,
one might have been able to derive more literary profit, treating it

82

with the classical emphasis, the rich romantic coloring, or the romanesque aesthetics.

But as we do not aspire to cause an effect but to paint things of the people such as they are, we have not wished to separate ourselves in one iota from naturalness and from truth. The language, except for aspirating the h's and eliminating the d's, is that of the Andalusian country people, just as are here their ideas, sentiments, and customs.

Many years of a study, made with constancy and with love, permit us to assure everyone who might argue the contrary that he is not as versed in the details as we are. (I, 143)

Fernán Caballero, then, at another earlier date in the nascent development of a Realistic novel, knows precisely what she wants to achieve: a truthful story, based securely on real facts in most instances and certainly in the essential parts, and a background of Andalusian scenery, characters, psychology, and speech, resulting from the author's observations. Again, her terminology is uncertain about the exact direction of this new novel—a new novel because the prior patterns of the eighteenth-century genre will be discarded, and the current vogues of Romantic and Gothic novels (a clear distinction exists for Fernán Caballero between these two phases of Romanticism) are too permeated with imagination and fantasy for the mid-nineteenth century. The surprising conclusion again is that Fernán Caballero with this short novel, well planned and well executed—and if the ideas in her few words to the readers correspond to the approximate date of composition of *The Family of Alvareda*, as Montesinos and Herrero so convincingly agree[4]—belongs chronologically with more notable relatives in the English and French literary families of Realism.

In the first part of her novel, the action starts in 1810 in the town of Dos Hermanas (Fernán Caballero as the Marquesa de Arco-Hermoso had of course acquired a residence in this Andalusian village near Sevilla) where two young men meet on a late afternoon. The two friends, about the same age of twenty and from Dos Hermanas, present different attitudes: Ventura, with a shotgun on his shoulder, "[whose] whole, graceful person gave forth a superabundance of life, force, energy" (I, 147); and Perico, with a hoe on his shoulder, "his brown eyes . . . lively, his look more tranquil, his mouth more serious, and his smile softer" (I, 147). Ventura is restless at home and wants to join his countrymen who are fighting Napoleon's soldiers, approaching swiftly and easily in their conquest of Spain; but Ventura's father opposes his son's departure. Also, Ventura is courting, not very decisively, Elvira, Perico's sister. Perico is in love with Rita, but his mother opposes the marriage; and he finally agrees to join the army with Ventura if his mother continues to refuse her permission for the wedding. Juan Alvareda, Perico's father, had died three years previously; and Perico has taken over the household responsibilities for Ana, his mother, and his sister, Elvira. Ana's refusal to approve her son's marriage to Rita is not based in reality upon the obstacle that they are cousins, since an ecclesiastical dispensation could be obtained without much delay; Ana objects strongly to Rita's personality which she sees in the future as the cause of marital unhappiness for her son. In the evening of the same day when the two youths discussed their problems about the future, Perico forces his mother to make the choice between his departure for military service and his marriage; and Ana, reluctantly, chooses the lesser of two evils— his selection of Rita as a wife—but the sorrowful mother warns him of his error. Friction between Ana and Rita, despite the intervention of the latter's mother, María, occurs before the wedding when the two women engage in some acrimonious remarks. Ventura's and Elvira's wedding is planned shortly thereafter, and the actual ceremony will take place before Perico's and Rita's marriage because of the latter's requirement of the papal dispensation. Marcela, Ventura's sister, arrives for her brother's wedding before she formally enters the novitiate. Rita shows an additional side to her increasingly antipathetic personality when she barely conceals her jealousy of Marcela—because the latter was the intended bride of Perico by both families before the girl decided to become a nun. On the wedding day, and unfortunately before the ceremony uniting Ventura and Elvira is celebrated, the French invaders, on their victorious march through Sevilla toward Cádiz, enter the village of Dos Hermanas. The families hide indoors, but a French grenadier enters the house and demands money, food, and drink. Pedro, trying to explain that he cannot provide the soldier with provisions and booty, is slapped in the face by the Fenchman; and Ventura, aroused by this insult to his father, kills the grenadier with his own saber. Ventura, hiding the corpse of the dead soldier, flees from Dos Hermanas; and Pedro, brokenhearted, watches his proud, quick-tempered son going into exile.

In 1816, when the second part begins, the two families of Dos Hermanas still remember often and unhappily the fatal day when Ventura vanished and about whom nothing has been heard. Perico and Rita married after Ventura's flight, and they now have two children; but Rita has not ceased to show antagonistic behavior toward her mother-in-law—and also her mother. Marcela, as a result of the traumatic events happening to her father and brother, has lost her mind. One night, during a severe storm, when the families are gathered together, Ventura arrives unexpectedly. He has suffered greatly during the War of Independence as a soldier and a prisoner; and his outlook on life, though tender toward the two families, has been altered for the worse because of the hardships, rough companions, and vulgar atmosphere of his surroundings. For example, Ventura no longer loves Elvira, whom he sees after so many years not as a prospective bride, but as a pale, thin, and unattractive girl, pitiful and withdrawn. Ventura and Rita fall in love, and they are accidentally discovered in the stable by Ana and María. Ana begs Rita to stop deceiving Perico, and a bitter quarrel between mother-in-law and daughter-in-law ends in a complete estrangement with the latter's insulting songs, previously directed at the former, now come to the fore in open conflict. On Christmas Day, Perico learns about the affair between his wife and Ventura when the children unknowingly repeat to the father a remark made by Ventura. Perico goes to the party where Ventura and Rita are dancing with each other, and a fight takes place between the two men with Ventura the easy winner. Pedro stops the quarrel, and the father takes his drunken son home where, on the following day, Ventura, repentant and ashamed, promises to marry Elvira without delay, and to stop his affair with Rita. Perico, however, enraged at his loss of honor and his humiliation before so many people at the Christmas party, determines upon revenge; and on that next day he shoots Ventura. The dying Ventura, with the priest and the notary present, admits his guilt for Perico's action and forgives him; but Pedro, in the procession with his dead son, passes Rita and angrily denounces her as the cause of the crime.

In the third part, Perico, in his desperate escape from Dos Hermanas—and from himself—is helped by a stranger who takes him to an inn and pays for all the expenses during the period of recuperation. This benefactor of Perico is, however, the leader of a gang of outlaws; and Diego sends one of his men, "El Presidiario" ("The Convict"), to bring Perico into the hideaway. Diego welcomes the apathetic Perico as a fellow criminal and member of the band of rogues. Meanwhile, at the village, a traveling mission of preachers has inspired forgiveness, mercy, and charity in the two suffering families as well as the other townspeople; and a reconciliation occurs, especially between Rita, confessing her responsibility for the tragedy, and Pedro, Ana, and María. No word is heard about Perico who, protected by Diego against the other bandits, ill-disposed to welcome "Perico el Triste" ("Perico the Sad"), has killed in an ambush the chief of a patrol. Diego explains to Perico that the latter has shot the Countess of Villaorán's son; and Perico is doubly brokenhearted because the Countess was a benefactress of his family and the son was one of his childhood companions. An old gypsy convinces the gang to rob a nearby church, but Perico frantically shouts that such a crime would be a sacrilege. His repeated protests against the planned theft irritate the others; but Diego, though unpersuaded by Perico's pleas, nevertheless prevents the robbers from harming him. Perico's shouts and the frightening atmosphere of the old church combine to terrify the bandits to such an extent that they abandon in haste the building. Their fears are compounded when they discover that "El Presidiario," left in charge of the horses, has disappeared; and the danger of treachery increases when the gypsy hag, declaring her innocence, nevertheless informs Diego and his men that the older son of the Countess of Villaorán is pursuing them to avenge his brother's murder. Diego's gang is successfully ambushed, thanks to the betrayal of "El Presidiario," and the Count of Villaorán is stunned upon learning that Perico, in addition to belonging to the band of outlaws, is the murderer of his brother. The irony of all these events, as the count explains in sorrow and anger, is that the murdered brother was searching for Perico in order to tell his boyhood friend that he has been pardoned, thanks to Ventura's and Pedro's forgiveness.

Perico's last days are spent in jail in Sevilla where he stoically accepts his punishment of death, after confessing his sins and admitting his remorse. The involved members of the two broken families, especially Rita, are shattered spiritually and psychologically after witnessing Perico's execution. Pedro and Ana die shortly thereafter, and Rita, convinced that her duty is to live for her children, leaves Dos Hermanas for the mountains and a lonely residence with some relatives. Reports from visitors state that Rita is only a shadow of her former self, tortured by remorseful, constant weeping. Finally, Melampo, the everpresent, loyal dog of the Alvareda family, dies almost immediately after Ana's funeral. These final results of the tragedy of the Alvaredas and their neighbors are related to travelers and visitors in Dos Hermanas as part of the local history—and as a lesson on the follies of human beings.

II *The Old, the True, and the Tried*

Very often, an exchange of letters between Fernán Caballero and Antoine de Latour, appearing first in the Madrid newspaper, *La España* (*Spain*) in 1856, is included after *The Family of Alvareda* as appendices to the novel. The interest is mainly historical and personal, and there are few direct references to the novel, with any consequent omission of the communications no integral loss to the main reading. However, the ideas in the letters show that Fernán Caballero enjoyed not only popularity, but also influence in her desire to restore true Spanish glories; and the lengthy descriptions about the restoration of the pennant of King Ferdinand III to the chapel at Dos Hermanas, mentioned in *The Family of Alvareda*, add immeasurably to the author's stature as deeply immersed in and enamored of Spain.[5] There is once again some faint resemblance to the efforts of the "Generation of 1898," particularly Azorín and Unamuno, in this pride and genuine patriotism in the authentic historical treasures of Spanish history. Also, Fernán Caballero's knowledge and investigations of her Andalusian residences, especially around Dos Hermanas, Sevilla, and Cadiz, were soundly rooted in long, objective studies, perhaps ̄ a legacy from Böhl von Faber's Hispanism. Sometimes, in the emphasis upon Fernán Caballero's aesthetic values as a novelist, these contributions are neglected and ignored. Like many foreigners (such as her acquaintance

of the years, 1828-1829, Washington Irving), Fernán Caballero
appreciated Spain more truly and profoundly than many natives,
although her vision was of course flawed by Romantic, idealizing,
and moral views. Her philosophical and ideological myopia,
however, did not prevent Fernán Caballero from associating history and tradition in the renaissance of popular faith, still valid
in the nineteenth-century miasma of Spanish internal politics,
which she grasped as the quicksand for any national founda-
tion.

Her literary views, of course, are closely allied with the above
issues of history and tradition; but, in these appendices to
The Family of Alvareda, Fernán Caballero emphasizes her
accurate rendition of observations and reports. "I shall answer
you," she writes to Latour, "that what I have narrated in the
novel, *La familia de Alvareda*, is the popular and verbal chronicle
that the people keep in the archives of their heart" (I, 203).
She clarifies one important change between *The Family of Alvareda* and *The Sea Gull*: the former is characterized by the absence
of many local color sketches and the few insertions are brief
cuadros de costumbres, more historical than in the vein of
folklore; and the latter novel is ironically often valued precisely
by literary history for the originality of linking *costumbrismo*
with the skeleton of a plot. Curiously, also, the criticism of possibly excessive *cuadros de costumbres* refers to *The Sea Gull*,
written about seventeen years after *The Family of Alvareda*.[6]
"But I have been told as much orally as in writing," she defends
her technique thus, "that those things were not necessary in the
novel; that those histories, those episodes, those digressions
caused interest to be lost in the narration and that they lengthened
it uselessly, that I had to yield and eliminate without mercy; I
only saved the story of the people of Dos Hermanas: on this
point I remained firm" (I, 204). Actually, since this sensitive (as
usual) defense belongs to 1856, Fernán Caballero, despite the
reference to Dos Hermanas, i.e., the novel, *The Family of
Alvareda*, may be obliquely referring to some contemporary
barbs against *The Sea Gull*. In her other novels, published before
1856, the *costumbrista* sketches generally are not as noticeable
as in *The Sea Gull*. Then, despite her assertion (quite correctly)
of the value of the local color sketches and the examples of
Andalusian folklore in that novel, Fernán Caballero restrained

herself from adding too many independent stories, legends, and historical items. Perhaps, then, like Cervantes, who in Part II of *Don Quijote* justified his use of intercalated novels, such as *La novela del curioso impertinente* (*The Tale of Ill-Advised Curiosity*) in Part I, but who did not include many independent novels in Part II, nevertheless, Fernán Caballero made a similar decision.[7]

Some familiar ideas also emerge in these appendices, such as her regret that the festive day on which the Duke of Montpensier, the loyal admirer of Fernán Caballero, brought the historical flag to a place of honor in Dos Hermanas was marked by a bullfight, the sole unfortunate feature of that occasion. The presence of aristocratic representatives, symbolizing the monarchical presence, and the rites recalling the medieval age of faith, for Fernán Caballero, evoked the spark of fervent enthusiasm for the old, the true, and the tried:

> The young Prince and Princess formed a worthy subject for an historical painting, with the Prince carrying the heavy staff while the delicate hands of the Princess carried the unfurled standard falling in graceful folds between both of them! Never was beauty of form united to sublimity of idea to compose such a group! Never did the present time find worthier representatives for a union across six centuries with a respectable past before that Lady at whose feet, for the second time, they brought the pennant offered by the inherited devotion of their glorious ancestor.... As for us, faithful interpreter of the traditions of that humble but interesting place, we, enthusiastic about everything saintly, good, and glorious—and of the charming, real poetry attached to these things—in the past just as in the present, never will be lost the remembrance of this day, its luster in our mind, its soft glow in our heart. (I, 206)

Here, then, are the poetry and the ideology of Fernán Caballero united in a passage of eminent purple prose, and here is likewise the absence of any realistic touch to modify the romantic glow. One of the purposes, consequently, of her novelistic venture in *The Family of Alvareda* is exactly this dogmatic, self-assured proclamation that Dos Hermanas and its inhabitants rate highly in the life of the nation, for the maintenance of the past rather than any hope for the future and present problems (omitted completely throughout the articles). This belief is further developed in Fernán Caballero's narrow interpretation of Spanish history with "my intelligence, my faculties, and my thoughts ... moved by love of religion and country (I, 207). Her explanations, however, demonstrate an accurate understanding of the pattern of Spanish decline and fall, admitted willingly and frankly. Spain, according to Fernán Caballero, rose to the peaks of power in many spheres; but the country has fallen on hard times, culminating in the disastrous nineteenth century. Her references in *The Family of Alvareda* to the humiliating insults of the French grenadier against the Spanish townspeople; and her main plot, pitting two families, logically harmonious, and struggling to live honorable, simple lives, engaged instead in almost fratricidal strife, the tragic consequence of violence, express perhaps unconsciously on Fernán Caballero's part a novelistic commentary on the historical and political events she referred to in these exchanges. More so than *The Sea Gull*, this first, firm direction in the Realistic novel employs a contemporary situation; and omitting any positive arguments for the symbolic interpretation of the background, the causes in the temperament and personality of her countrymen for a portion of their tragedy seem clearly indicated by the author. Historically, in the simplistic view of Fernán Caballero, the Spanish decadence is the consequence of a mysterious destiny, or, in her orthodox spirit (though not overtly stated here), the will of God.

Is there hope for the Spanish people and the national future? Again, the replies of Fernán Caballero are found in the life of her townspeople in *The Family of Alvareda*: "love of home and family"; "reconstruction, a work of gold and of powerful men, of spirit and of culture"; "monarchs and princes with love of country, with zest for improvements, with adherence to the glories of religion and history" (I, 208). Her premises are essentially correct, and the keen observations, of which Fernán Caballero took pride as a writer, have served her faithfully and constructively. She, then, is all too cognizant of the present; but her solutions are mired in the past. Spain does not need to change so much as to grapple with the proverbial hoops of steel the virtues and traditions of the past. The three sinners, rather than criminals for Fernán Caballero's religious and moral philosophy, illustrate not only personal tragedies when transgressions are committed against the law and the commandments, but also the widening breach in public, social, and family relations as a consequence of their actions. Fortunately, however, in *The Family of Alvareda*, the author has effectively camouflaged her lessons and didacticism—at least in the first two parts—with a dynamic, fast-moving action and psychologically motivated, realistic characters.[8]

III *Novel and* Comedia

Montesinos has referred to *The Family of Alvareda* as "a true Andalusian drama,"[9] and the tone of passionate violence, so prominent in Fernán Caballero's novel, has been compared to García Lorca's theme in *Bodas de sangre* (*Blood Wedding*).[10] The Duque de Rivas, in a prologue to the book version of the novel, praised the author's skillful employment of dramatic techniques, such as "a true action, very simple, coordinated with great taste and very successfully"; and "the dialogues are admirable, and the opportunity by which common popular songs, innocent, pious preoccupations of our people, religious sentiments are inserted in them."[11] Also, the structure of Fernán Caballero's novel resembles the dramatic art: "The incidents are imagined with great truth and simplicity, and so well connected that they carry the reader to the dénouement, without the slightest trouble and without his interest being lost for a moment."[12] The Duque de Rivas, of course, won his place in Spanish literature, principally as a dramatist; and his theatrical production of *Don Alvaro o la fuerza del sino* (*Don Alvaro or the Force of Destiny*) in 1835 carried the day for Romanticism against Neoclassical opponents—and gave Verdi the basis for his very popular opera, *La forza del destino* (*The Force of Destiny*). One may likewise recall Böhl von Faber's defense and advocacy of the classical Spanish drama for the daughter's knowledge of the *comedia*.

The three parts of *The Family of Alvareda* correspond in several ways to the theory of the *comedia* of the Golden Age or, at least, as Lope de Vega attempted to define the dramatic genre in *Arte nuevo de hacer comedias* (*New Art of Writing Plays*) in 1609. Fernán Caballero, persistently endeavoring to escape the classification of novels for her books,[13] certainly found in *The Family of Alvareda* a successful formula, despite the lack of any sure evidence that she definitely imitated the classical theater.

The first two parts of the novel offer the widest appeal, while the third part shows Fernán Caballero too concerned with the moral and didactic lessons to be acquired from Perico's—and Rita's—tragedy. In the first part, all the main characters are introduced, the conflicts are established, the action is rapid, and the section ends on an exciting, unexpected turn, with the arrival of the French grenadier, his murder, and Ventura's flight. There are few digressive elements, a minimum of description, and the local color sketches, stories, and legends, short and narrative in conception and execution. The exception occurs in the sixth chapter where, in the longest digression, Fernán Caballero relates the "Crónica popular y verbal de Dos Hermanas" ("Popular and Verbal Chronicle of Dos Hermanas"); but she is very insistent in a footnote that "the person who writes this . . . heard it from the mouth of that woman, and she wrote it immediately in the same terms and very words, without adding or subtracting," and "if indeed the background is a very known thing, it is of great interest for the one who studies the temper of the people to see the clear and precise manner with which they conceive things, the nobleness with which they tell them, and especially, the religious sentiment which shines and predominates in them" (I, 159). In short, the old woman, serving as the narrator in this sixth chapter, represents not legend but history, although of course the "chronicle" belongs more properly to the legendary rather than the historical. But the difference for Fernán Caballero exists only theoretically; both legend and history are merged into what Unamuno will later call the *intrahistoria* ("intrahistory") of a people. "The good old woman," in Fernán Caballero's repeated phrase, serves therefore as the artistic link between the story and the history and myth about the founding of Dos Hermanas.

The chapters of this first part are short, and each chapter is almost a contained unit with a scene, usually of conflict or confrontation. For example, the first chapter depicts Ventura and Perico, friends and intended in-laws, but with very distinct personalities; the second chapter introduces the women in the story with some hints of Rita's antipathetic nature; the third chapter presents the argument between Perico and his mother about the former's marriage to Rita; the fourth chapter offers a lesson in country wit and wisdom in the marriage contract terms, argued by Ana and Pedro; the fifth chapter is another light, semihumorous depiction of Ana and Pedro on a trip to Alcalá; and the seventh chapter, ending the first part, provides a scene of violence with the historical introduction of the French invasion. The sixth chapter is the most placid episode of this part, with no action of any consequence to the plot—giving thereby the possible omission of this chapter from the novel—and the only importance residing in the above-mentioned chronicle of Dos Hermanas and in one of the author's attacks on "the free woman" of her time. There is a successful utilization of the serious and the comic in the first part; and the fourth and fifth chapters relieve the growing tensions caused by Perico's coming marriage and the approaching interruption of the marriage by the French soldier. The dialogue, the main thrust of Fernán Caballero's technique in this part, contributes a natural, realistic, conversational quality, reflecting the particular character's traits and attitude. The use of proverbs and regionalisms adds to Fernán Caballero's success in the employment of language, especially in her disregard of any romantic discourses.

The second part follows equally a dramatic curve of rising action, conflicts erupting initially as psychological and finally as physical; and the section terminates with not only murder, but the flight of a main character. Indeed, the parallels between the first two parts of the novel reveal a well-structured organization by the author; she has effectively repeated the same patterns of an increasingly rising confrontation among her characters. The second part is better motivated and psychologically more realistic—and contemporary—than the first part. In the first part, Fernán Caballero is essentially looking backward to the patriotic, national pride in the War of Independence, certainly a favorite among Spanish authors and a legitimate source of literary endeavors, but the French grenadier's sudden appearance is somewhat of a *deus ex machina* despite Ventura's and Perico's earlier discussion in the first chapter about joining the army to fight the invaders in 1810. Both parts, building up then to high points of violence, bloodshed, murder, and flight, differ markedly, however: the Romantic aura, especially in the first chapter of the second part, supplies a Gothic setting with a raging storm as the opening physical feature, soon to be reflected in the tempestuous, personal relations of the families in Dos Hermanas.

The *cuadros de costumbres* are almost absent in the middle division, but the use of dances and songs, woven ably into the plot progression, renders local color and reflects Andalusian folklore—those two additions of Fernán Caballero proudly present in her novels and stories. The first chapter, as in the introductory episode of the first part, serves as the presentation of all the characters once again united with Ventura's Romantic return; and, ironically, all seems placid and prosperous for the future. But in the second chapter, Ventura's adventures as a soldier have stirred Rita's imagination, and her interest in him slowly emerges. This mood of *tempo lento* vanishes in the third chapter when the first conflict takes place in the discovery of Ventura and Rita alone in the stable, and the die is cast for trouble. This trouble develops in the bitter dialogue between Ana and Rita about the latter's infidelity; and Fernán Caballero, briefly and forcefully, achieves a masterly use of dialogue in the vocal clashes. The three following chapters continue the mounting sense of disaster with Perico's ire aroused by Rita's absence and affair; with the argument between the two men, balanced skillfully by the succinct analyses of their individual motives, reactions, thoughts, and behavior; with Ventura's abandonment of emotion for reason and, unfortunately, Perico's change from a reasonable man to a person of irrational vengeance—a convincing demonstration of characterization and literary technique. Once more, *The Family of Alvareda* concludes in a manner very reminiscent of the *comedia* by the dramatic arrival of Ventura's body in the street of Dos Hermanas, the residents gathering in shocked witness of the tragedy, the traumatic effects upon the women in the story, and Pedro's melodramatic outburst against Rita at the moment, theatrically staged, of his uncovering of his son's blood-stained corpse—all accomplished with an economy of words, a general absence of description, and the emphasis upon the events speaking for themselves.

There is a general critical consensus that the third part of *The Family of Alvareda* is the weakest, artistically and thematically, of the three actions because Fernán Caballero succumbs to her cardinal sin as a writer by allowing ideology to supersede aesthetics.[14] Also, the Romantic and Gothic traits, which she opposed in a novel and by which she frequently classified the whole genre, predominate in the last part. Almost the entire argument revolves

around Perico's fate as an outcast from society—a Romantic hero
in many ways—and the first chapter, conveniently staged during
another of Fernán Caballero's favorite storms, also introduces
a darling of Romanticism, the good, noble bandit. Based apparently on an historical figure, Diego Corrientes, a "Robin Hood"
of Spain like the Roque Guinart whom Don Quijote and Sancho
meet on their journey to Barcelona, the Diego of Fernán Caballero's creation proves faithful to her stress upon realism and
observation, as she interpreted these aspects, with the Romantic characterization an influence from the past and a help for
her theses. The Romantic contrast appears in the figure of "El
Presidiario," who serves as the antithesis of Diego. For example,
Diego saves and protects Perico, while "El Presidiario" is openly
opposed to the newcomer's entry into the ranks of the gang; and,
Judas-like (if the Romantic analogy secularizing the New Testa-
ment is pursued), "El Presidiario" betrays Diego who accepts
heroically and stoically his fate. If the third part of the novel
seems to veer sharply in the direction of the Romantic drama,
nevertheless the analogies with the *comedia* still invite a valid
comparison because, as critics have recognized consistently, the
resemblances between the Spanish theaters of Romanticism and
the Golden Age are many and important. The abortive robbery
of the church in the seventh chapter is highly melodramatic, and
the heightening of emotion and fear by natural phenomena, such
as the moonbeam suddenly appearing through a window and
falling at the feet of a statue dedicated to the Virgin Mary, foreshadows happenings in several *leyendas* (legends) of Bécquer,
a fellow Sevillian of Fernán Caballero, and whom she mentions
offhandedly elsewhere in her works.

Structurally, also, this third part continues the winning formula of the two preceding parts by constructing slowly and
evenly an approaching confrontation, necessarily violent and
disastrous, this time by the fact that criminals are involved in
robberies and ambushes, between the law and the gang, culminating in Perico's sentence of death. The pace of the rapidly
changing scenes is sustained easily by the variety of Perico's
adventures, the danger concomitant in each chapter, and the
characters themselves who reflect the atmosphere of desperate
rogues in unsavory enterprises. Likewise, although Perico's
fate is sealed by Fernán Caballero's emphasis upon his solitary,

depressed condition and state of mind, the exact measures by which her tragic character will be punished follow logically and in an artistically mature form from each prior chapter. The outcome of the individual scene is uncertain, with the possibility in all instances that Diego's band may be successful or that the authorities may apprehend the outlaws. However, each successive step in Perico's decline and fall is never arrested by the chance of salvation. Still, his redemption is at hand at the moment he opposes the church desecration, when first proposed by the Celestina-like gypsy, is confirmed by his role in preventing the robbery by the shouts, and is finally triumphant by confession and absolution before execution. Of course, the heavy veneer of moralistic, religious, and theological redemption by Fernán Caballero predominates throughout the vignettes, but the psychological study of Perico is still well motivated, persuasive, and realistic. The epilogue, a final sermon on the tragedy of the Alvareda family, returns to a mode of realism, familiar in the first two parts; and Melampo (the word is theatrical in origin and symbolic in the novel, referring to a prompter's candle or light in the theater) contributes by his death a melodramatic, sentimental, and instructive note to this novel.

IV *The Threefold Background*

If the structure of *The Family of Alvareda* resembles significantly and skillfully a theatrical piece, and especially the *comedia* with Romantic devices, the background is nonetheless composed of the threefold interest of Fernán Caballero in observation, realism, and *costumbrismo*. The novel certainly offers a major advance in the Realistic movement with not only photographic reproduction—the novelist's main claim in her view—but another contribution in nineteenth-century Realism appears in characterization, the psychological distinctions of individuals, and the rudimentary comprehension glimpsed at times of the vagaries of human nature and actions.

Although the quantity of local color sketches as brief insertions in *The Family of Alvareda* is small (particularly with reference to *The Sea Gull*, as indicated previously), the novel is certainly a *costumbrista* work, explained concisely by Fernán Caballero in "a word to the reader." The main example, the history and legend about Dos Hermanas, is matched by the description of the village's background at the novel's beginning and Fernán Caballero, once again contrasting Romantic and Realistic concepts, defends her theory on the first page: "In order to make this village, which has the reputation of being very ugly, a picturesque and showy place, it would be necessary to have an imagination which might create, and the person who describes it here only paints" (I, 145). The setting is economically detailed, and Fernán Caballero loses no time in introducing her characters and her story so that the *costumbrista* values of *The Family of Alvareda* derive from the real-life plot and the Andalusian characters. In short, the author has not granted herself the pleasure, as will her regionalist successors, such as Pereda, of composing very long, poetically-phrased geographical descriptions. Her artistry in these aspects brings the book to the high level of the novelistic Realism of Galdós and Valera.

In fact, Fernán Caballero's portrayal of her characters provides a surprising realism and subtle criticism of Spanish society, particularly the fate of countrywomen, as, for example, in this glimpse: "At this moment good old María arrived. María was older than her sister-in-law, and although she was just about sixty years old, her smallness and thinness, and the speed with which village women age, made her appear a great deal older" (I, 150). Here is a sharp, vivid picture, thankfully uncomplicated and unspoiled by any sermonizing and moral conclusions. The dialogue can be equally effective and revealing when, in Perico's argument with his mother about marriage, the conversation is interrupted by a mutually silent reaction from parent and child:

> Upon saying these words, the noble woman, choking with tears, went into her bedroom in order to hide them from her son.
>
> Perico, who loved his mother with tenderness as much as with veneration, made a movement as if to stop her; he tried to speak, but his timidity, joined to his confusion, dulled his faculties; he did not find his voice, he remained an instant, indecisive. At once he got up abruptly, passed his hand across his moist forehead, and left. (I, 152)

But the opposite effect is apparent when Fernán Caballero allows her piety and undoubtedly sincere orthodoxy to generalize about one character: "Pedro was accompanied by his daughter, who threw herself around María's neck with that tender openness of nuns and children, that is to say, of human beings whose heart has not been bruised, wounded, or turned cold through contact with society" (I, 158). The impression, of course, is simplistic and unconvincing; and a step backward from Realism is taken by such repeated defects as these intrusive, subjective generalizations. If Fernán Caballero had adhered to an objective conclusion about the religious vocation, which she achieves in this analysis of Marcela's vocation, she would have remained firmly in the Realistic mold: "She wanted to be a nun, not because of religious exaltation, but because of pleasure; not with misanthropy, but with joy of heart; not through lack of finding in the world a convenient position or place, which many believe the cause for taking the veil, but because she found this place, this position preferentially in her convent" (I, 159). Both vocations, the true and the false, are compared and contrasted impartially; and Marcela's religious calling is rendered plausible and authentic by this realistic survey. Then, in the following paragraph, this insight into psychology and objectivity about the reasons for ecclesiastical vocations is marred by a prolonged attack, rather fanatical and prolix, on *la mujer libre* ("the free woman") of the nineteenth century:

This is what many persons do not understand or pretend not to understand. Everything is understood in the world, all the vices, all the irregularities, the most atrocious inclinations, even that of the cannibals; but that of the tranquil and withdrawn life, without care of the present or the future, is denied. Everything is believed in the world; one believes in the free woman, the morality of theft, the philanthropy of the guillotine, men in the moon, and other puffs (lies) as the English say, or canards (false reports), as our neighbors say or *bolas* (humbug) and *patrañas* (fake stories), as we say. The skeptical satyr called world swallows all of it, because there is nothing so credulous as incredulity, as superstitious as irreligion. But one does not believe in the instincts of purity, in modest desires, in humble hearts, in religious sentiments—certainly not that. The existence of these is a puff, a canard, a humbug that is not accepted; this Minotaur is not so gullible. For those philosophers who pretend to guide opinion, a nun is either a sacrificial victim or a monster removed from the laws of nature and its sacred instincts. Noble and elevated are certainly your sacred instincts if they engender the free woman and deny the religious woman, submissive and chaste. (I, 159)

Fortunately, this is a rare passage in *The Family of Alvareda*, but the paragraph illustrates the handicap in Fernán Caballero's novelistic ideal and explains why she failed to become in literary history a Balzac, Dickens, or Scott. Her passages of literary realism predominate in this novel, and she can arouse a mood and a reaction in harmony with her intentions, moral and didactic, by observation and narration. For example, in what one may call Perico's part (since he is at the center of the third part), the analogy between his condition and that of the setting stands out clearly, sharply: "At this moment the clouds parted; the moonlight, clear and whitish, spread everywhere like a cape of transparent snow. Everything comes outside the mysteries of the shadows. In his eyes Ecija is introduced, asleep in her valley like a white bird in its nest. He looks upward in the direction of the mysterious outcry. How horrible! He sees five human heads upon five posts! They are what is sending forth the pitiful moaning, like a warning from the dead to the living" (I, 185). In a footnote, Fernán Caballero, as if to defend herself against a possible charge of utilizing the imagination, or the Romantic, to create such an effect, adds knowingly that "several people testify to this frightful phenomenon, explained naturally by the noise that the wind forms, going through the passages of the throat, mouth, and ears of the heads placed there" (I, 185).

The other weakness of Fernán Caballero in the use of a threefold background of observation, realism, and *costumbrismo* consists of her compulsion to attack opposing ideas by interrupting the story. These digressions, more revealing and explanatory about the author than the virtuous moralizing, could impede seriously the execution of a successful novel. Diego's portrait, for example, combines happily an acceptable view of his personality, and at the same time, remarks on Romanticism that find their way within the body of the paragraph:

Diego felt himself attracted to that man [i.e., Perico] who had saved his life, that man who was good and honorable, because the harsh and rough nature of Diego was strong and noble, and he had not descended to the worst degree of wickedness, which is to hate the good. Without coming to the novelistic exaggeration which makes a bandit or a pirate a hero, we are still beyond the classic puritanism which makes a thief such a monster, not having a single human atom, denying thus, in honor of established morality and the intransigent police, the known deeds of valor, generosity, and nobility seen in the leaders of such gangs. The fact alone of having become leaders of similar men proves an immense superiority, keeping a mastery, supported and sustained in nothing but by his own strength. (I, 191)

Instead of detracting from Fernán Caballero's reputation as a writer, such passages, balanced, impartial, modern in any view of contemporary criminology, contribute not only thoughts on the Romantic currents, but also, subjectively, on practical social and personal attitudes. Removed from too close an embrace with the Church, Fernán Caballero is refreshingly—and surprisingly—advanced for her time; and her lapses into dogmatic, strident arguments often accompany scenes and descriptions in churches, monasteries, as well as with monks and nuns. The most noticeable example of this tendency occurs in the attempted robbery of the church by Diego's band; the most compelling, though extensive, treatment of theological, orthodox doctrines is found in Perico's imprisonment and last moments of life.

Critical impartiality and justice call attention to adverse points of *The Family of Alvareda,* points which commentators have in fact regretted consistently for having lowered the reputation and importance of the work.[15] But the merits of Fernán Caballero's Realism certainly stand out in this novel in two modern, major ways: the *costumbrismo* and the characterization. Some instances of the local color sketches have been indicated already, and these instances perhaps overshadow the less conspicuous qualities of the Andalusian background. The songs express in particular the humor, wit, and wisdom of the peasants of Andalucía; and these *coplas* find wide usage as an original contribution of Fernán Caballero's art. She recognizes the importance of this Andalusian expression:

Rita, according to the custom of the country, began to sing.
Among persons of Andalusian stock, each one has in his memory such an archive of songs, so varied in their concepts, that it would be difficult for someone to be given something to express and not to find in a song the way to do it. (I, 174)

Rita, appealingly adept at *coplas* despite their intended target in the more virtuous Ana, contributes several barbs, which
still sound relevant in this age-old lament about some marital
woes: "Oh for the luck/of Adam and Eve,/ who never knew/
a father-in-law or a mother-in-law," and "A wagon is full/of
mothers- and sisters-in-law:/what a fine load/for hell!" (I, 174).
Variety of metrical form and a content, ranging from the comical
to the religious, also figure in the first two parts of the novel.
Since the action of the third part, with the exception of the tragic
epilogue (hardly an appropriate place for *coplas*), occurs outside
Dos Hermanas, symbol of regionalism and local color material,
there are no songs in this last section.

In the chapter where Ana and Pedro do a great deal of hard
bargaining, in a vein reminiscent of the legendary New England
Yankees, and finally make a deal—"discussing thus, they settled
the bases for the contract, remaining before as after, the best
friends in the world" (I, 154)—the whole scene is pleasantly
interspersed with proverbs, witticisms, and probing remarks
about finances, all in the uniquely Andalusian manner. Likewise,
the following sequence, in which Pedro outtalks, and somewhat
outmaneuvers, the other travelers at the inn, is replete with the
same light bantering, with a sharp-edged intent if the listener
wishes to pursue the possibilities. The first greetings to Pedro
and María provide innocent amusement and surprising candor
with no insults intended.

"Uncle! Where are you going with that face from Lent?" asked
one.

"Aunt!" said the other. "Is the church still standing where they
baptized you?"

"Aunt!" said another. "Do you still remember your wedding night?"

"Uncle!" asked the fourth, "Are you going to Alcalá to take your
wedding vows with that young girl?"

"No," answered Pedro, slowly getting off his donkey. "Because for
that, I am waiting to come of age and for the girl just to grow up."

"Aunt!" continued the soldiers. "Do you want us to help you to
get off that gift horse?"

"That's the best thing you can do, my boys," answered the good
woman.

The soldiers approached and helped her to climb down in an
attentive and kind way. (I, 156)

Even in the other inn, where Perico is recovering from his exhaustion after being rescued by Diego, the innkeeper and his wife, although the tone is fearful and hostile about the conditions surrounding their unwelcome guest, exchange comments with piquancy, especially about the disadvantages of the discovery and colonization of the New World. The remarks, of course, open a new vista upon Fernán Caballero's vision of empire-building ambitions of her countrymen; and her conclusions (unfavorable about war throughout her writings) against the expenditures of human and material resources may be a reflection at the time of composition of *The Family of Alvareda* that the American empire, lost through wars of independence, has been a liability. Certainly the salty remarks of the innkeeper's wife reflect adversely upon the desire for imperialistic enterprises, whereas her husband defends rather naively, and weakly, the values of overseas possessions. Fernán Caballero shows herself perceptive and prophetic about this political issue, and once again, she shows some affinities, unintentionally probably, with the critical spirit of Larra, the precursor, and Costa, Ganivet, and Unamuno in their turn-of-the-century attacks on Spanish errors and blunders in expansionist dreams.

Fernán Caballero's characterization in *The Family of Alvareda,* while more limited to one class of people than to the broader areas of society in *The Sea Gull,* nevertheless presents some similarities with personages of the later novel. Rita and Marisalada, in particular, are molded from the same stamp; and Fernán Caballero in *The Family of Alvareda* first evolved the type of woman who will appear in a pattern in many works, reaching an apogee in *La farisea* (*The Woman of the Pharisees*), one of her last and most popular books. Rita, like many of these literary creations, is primarily noted by "her cold heart," a repeated phrase of Fernán Caballero. The pattern for Rita (as for Marisalada) is initially: "the haughty, harsh, and determined condition that her daughter, Rita, showed since a child; these bad qualities had been then developed unhindered. Her character was violent, her impressions fiery, and her heart cold" (I, 149); a strange ennui before the wedding which she had previously urged: "Only Rita had a bored and indifferent air" (I, 162); a passionate, immediate attraction for a strongly masculine, romantic partner in love: "Since Ventura entered, she had not taken her sight from the dashing young man, whose moustache, uniform, and military bearing suited him haughtily" (I, 170); a total, emotional involvement: "Rita knew no restraint, and military life had been for Ventura a school for bad habits" (I, 173); a downfall with the realization of her mistakes: "She was the unhappiest of the three women because she was the guilty one" (I, 191); and at last a complete breakdown: "Some compassionate people took away the prostrate Rita and led her to an inn. Her condition was terrible, the convulsions shattering her allowed few instants of consciousness; and in these she showed her desperation in such a frightful way, that it was necessary to subdue her like an insane person" (I, 200). At the end, however, there is one difference between Rita and Marisalada: the former is completely repentant, illustrating more sharply Fernán Caballero's insistence upon the moral lessons; and the latter, although humiliated and humbled by her disgrace, still hurls invective at the taunting Momo. But these two heroines— or antiheroines—establish the author as headed in the direction of psychological development of character.

Of course, most of the characters, as in *The Sea Gull*, represent Andalusian types rather than individual actors in the story. Fernán Caballero's women are depicted in general more sympathetically and praiseworthily than the men, and she is especially devoted to the concept of the mother, loyal, suffering, humble, and wise. As a grandmother, the female character holds together the family by serving as a link between the children, to whom she relates the folklore and tradition of Andalucía, and the mother, sometimes unconcerned about preservation of the past. Ana and María in *The Family of Alvareda* bear close resemblances, similar to the portrait of Aunt María in *The Sea Gull*. These examples have their origin in Fernán Caballero's idealization of life: the older generation symbolizes the past, and the conservative, traditional viewpoints stress that a younger generation looks to the elders for advice and follows closely, with few if any missteps (and any changes would be usually erroneous for the author) from the guidelines already established. Here seems the ideological concept for another pattern in Fernán Caballero's work; and again, ideology has superimposed itself upon the literary creation. Nonetheless, the types provide warm-

hearted appeal and readily acceptable realism; and they are
indeed representative of not only Andalusian country folk but
of universal qualities. In this manner, by avoiding the extremes
of Romantic, sentimental characters (such as Stein in *The Sea
Gull*), Fernán Caballero has with success grafted local color
portrayals to the body of her story.

In drawing her masculine characters, Fernán Caballero strove
to render in Pedro a personage equivalent to the women, Ana
and María. The two antagonists, Ventura and Perico, show
another side to this coin of the Andalusian peasant: they are
honorable, loyal, and courageous, of course; but they are quick-
tempered, emotional, and compelled to live up to a code of
honor, as in the *comedia*. Ironically, this defense of honor is
exactly the precipitating cause of the tragedy; and the pride
of both former friends also leads irrevocably to their mutual
downfall and death. There are indeed in *The Family of Alvareda*
no real villains (with the exception of the minor participant,
"El Presidiario"), and Rita's contrition and suffering redeem
her sufficiently from that classification as well as the previous
forgiveness of the families after the preaching mission has
aroused in them the spirit of charity. Diego, of course, is truly
noble and honorable, especially at the time of his capture. In
fact, Fernán Caballero, in the characterization of this earlier
and first novel, has attained an equivalent level of literary
psychology in her personages that she reached in *The Sea Gull*,
about seventeen years later. Also, her characters are more in
accord with regional, local color individuals; and she has interestingly avoided the pitfalls of Romanticism—against which she
wrote so emphatically—in all the principal actors, although
traces of the Romantic techniques exist in other aspects of the
book, particularly the third part. Her success at such a date,
around 1828, is remarkable, as Montesinos and Herrero note,[16]
and as other investigators have so amply documented.

V *Genesis and Birth of* The Family of Alvareda

This documentation about the evolution of *The Family of
Alvareda,* in addition to the revelations about personal artistic
inspiration and methods, proves that Fernán Caballero utilized
sources not so much from readings, parental influences, and the

cultural ambiance, as from observation and direct involvement. The first materials for this novel came from a true incident narrated to Fernán Caballero who, as the Marquesa de Arco-Hermoso, came to Dos Hermanas; and, in fact, she indicates this explanation at the beginning of the epilogue (concealing as the familiar trait of her authorship her identity): "Years after what took place the marqués de *** went to spend some time on an estate at Dos Hermanas" (I, 201). She continues in this brief epilogue to insert her second husband as the listener of some of the events, and she remains outside the action completely. However, this early example of Fernán Caballero's desire for anonymity does not lessen the proof that she accompanied the Marqués de Arco-Hermoso during the narration. Without accepting completely Coloma's report, though apparently rather accurate, the truth is more concisely that "the impression was so painful, so profound, caused in her mind by the reference made by a countryman about the principal event which forms the argument of *The Family of Alvareda*, that without realizing what she was doing, only through mere curiosity and in order not to forget details of such an interesting story, she began to write about it on the same night they told it to her, and although in very different form from what they gave to her, she had it finished before going to bed at daybreak."[17]

However, Fernán Caballero's role in the novelistic construction, though based upon the truthful reenactment of the facts as they were narrated in her presence (her immediate writing of the events assures a high degree of accuracy, one of her constant aims, in any case), has been demonstrated as more than that of an amanuensis. A partial explanation for the interest in the genesis of *The Family of Alvareda* resides of course in Washington Irving's involvement, at least accidental, but probably of some decisiveness. At first considered as a myth or a tradition, Washington Irving's knowledge of and interest in the story have been proved after Antoine de Latour mentioned the American, without any evidence as a reader, in an 1857 article: "She had written *The Family of Alvareda* under the lively emotion of narration from a witness. Then she had given it to be read by Washington Irving who was by chance passing through Sevilla and the approval of the famous compatriot of Fenimore Cooper had satisfied her ambition."[18] Irving was very favorably im-

pressed: he outlined the main points of the plot, sketchily but
coherently; and the principal difference is that the third part,
laconically stated as "turned robber," apparently then did not
exist as a complete set of adventures.[19] Ironically, this third
part (the later result of Fernán Caballero's imagination) is of
course the weakest part. "This third part, it should be noted,
is much the least convincing part of the novel," argue Hespelt
and Williams, "It is full of improbable situations, bad psychology, and literary conventions, and is an excellent proof of the
fact that Fernán Caballero was at her best only when telling
the 'truth.' "[20] Although not as revealing as the implications
about the third part, the notes show nevertheless that changes
were later made:

> The story as Irving sketches it has all the traits of a real incident in
> village life, and the personal note concerning the Marchioness's own
> part in the affair seems to lend it even greater authenticity.
>
> It is, perhaps, unnecessary to discuss in detail all the changes
> which the anecdote underwent between the date of Irving's call
> and the publication of The Family of Alvareda in 1849, but certain
> important differences in the two versions of the story will immediately
> occur to the reader familiar with the novel. In the later version the
> alignment of characters has been changed; the "soldier," Ventura,
> becomes the only son of his father; the "husband," Perico, the sole
> support of a widowed mother; a secondary plot telling of the love
> affair between Ventura and Perico's sister has been added; the back-
> ground of the French invasion has been sketched in; two very
> dramatic scenes—Ventura's home-coming from the wars and Perico's
> discovery of the adultery—have been inserted; the unforgivable insult
> is no longer, "Tu no has (!) vergüenza," but the epithets, "mata-
> langostas . . . cobarde . . . gallina, criado bajo las faldas de tu madre."[21]

In these two parts, then, Fernán Caballero's intervention has
added a more dramatic and more interesting quality to the
framework of the plot, as originally related; and she has happily
maintained a realistic, objective, and very plausible development
in the action, without yielding to the romantic, moralizing under-
currents of Perico's downfall in the last part. Her artistry is
certainly vindicated in these worthwhile additions and alterations.

The next step in the growth of the novel, shortly after Irving
heard and summarized the basic plot, has been traced to its
first draft: "Such is the plot of the anecdote as Irving remem-

bered it after his memorable conversation with the marchioness. If our conjectures are correct, the story had grown three months later to a full-length manuscript novel. A number of scenes and episodes incidental to the main plot had been added and the main plot itself had been brought to a conclusion which would satisfy the requirements of fiction by rendering poetic justice to all the characters."[22] This manuscript, though not identified by name or title as *The Family of Alvareda,* was apparently read by Irving two months later: "I have lately had the pleasure of reading the manuscript of the Marchioness of Arco Hermoso; although written in so small a hand, I was so much interested with it that I hurried through it in the course of a night and a day. I have since re-read parts of it more quietly and leisurely. It contains a great variety of very interesting and characteristic sketches and observations, thrown off with great freedom and spirit."[23] Even if the logical explanation should be perhaps incorrect that Irving is referring to *The Family of Alvareda,* there is at least no doubt that Doña Cecilia's American visitor was sufficiently informed by her and greatly impressed by her first literary efforts to record in detail facts and reactions. On her side, the Marquesa de Arco-Hermoso, probably flattered to no little extent by the famous author's words, continued to discuss and reveal openly story possibilities, anecdotes, legends, etc. This next stage of the novel (whether read or not read by Irving) provides nevertheless the basis for a profitable comparison with the printed versions in *El Heraldo* and in the *Obras completas*; and this *Historieta Traducida del Alemán de una Joven Española* (*Anecdote Translated from the German of a Young Spanish Girl*) may be again of rather decisive importance in Spanish literature of the nineteenth century: "It is not at all incredible that the *Historieta* may have come into existence as a result of Irving's interest and enthusiasm; that Fernán had 'had the goodness to write out' its contents during the months which had elapsed since his first call; that he is, therefore, directly responsible for it and indirectly responsible for the regeneration of the Spanish novel in the nineteenth century. But this, again, is not capable of definite proof."[24]

At any rate, the *Historieta* shows that Fernán Caballero did work extensively on what by now is really beyond the classification of an "anecdote" or a "short history"—as she must have also understood—and is within the genre of the novel. In fact, the *Historieta* is considerably longer than the present novel, according to the accepted *Obras completas,* and is likewise longer and different in many ways from the serial form in *El Heraldo.* Perhaps, then, Fernán Caballero's previously mentioned insistence that she had omitted the local color sketches, stories, and legends of *The Family of Alvareda* refers to the editing she did before the novel's appearance in *El Heraldo;* and it is possible to consider the suggestions, including further cuts in the texts, by editors, such as Ochoa.[25] There is, indeed, throughout the correspondence of Fernán Caballero a constant strain of criticism about editorial revisions, with even the Duque de Rivas the source of irritation on her part for some minor differences in *The Family of Alvareda*—for which he had of course written a eulogistic, prestigious review.[26] Also, another show of Fernán Caballero's reluctance to stand too openly in full view of her audiences is in the marked difference in the epilogues of the *Historieta* and the later, standard versions of the novel. In the *Historieta,* the Marquesa de Arco-Hermoso reveals herself as a writer and as a woman: she asks many questions about the details of the family's tragedy; probes for motives; considers the facts quickly and analytically; and expresses herself with a great deal of feeling, warmth, and emotion, attempting indeed to intervene subtly and charitably. The critical question, tantalizing and rhetorical, may be posed: Which of the two epilogues might be a more effective, literary conclusion? The *Historieta* draft is longer, personal, summarizing, autobiographical; and the present arrangement is very concise, staccato, and dramatic, because of Melampo's death after Ana's funeral.

As for the parts, Part I essentially has undergone few changes in the definitive serial and book version; and in general, Fernán Caballero has only shortened some of the more detailed actions, such as the "Marcela motif," where Marcela has now receded into the background as a minor character.[27] Otherwise, the chapters, episodes, and even stories of Dos Hermanas remain intact with only narrative excisions to shorten the text. With Part II, the omissions are striking, especially in the extensive disappearance of Fernán Caballero's contributions, according to the usual points of literary view, to the modern Spanish novel. Again, Hespelt, who studied the unpublished *Historieta,* must be accepted fully as the only source: "Part II has undergone in the course of its history much more profound changes than Part I. Of the fourteen chapters which it covers in the manuscript volume, the first six (Chapters 8-13) are composed of material extraneous to the main plot of the novel. They present 'folk-lore scenes' and long digressions in the form of 'ejemplos' and other stories. The thread of the main plot is not resumed until Chapter 14 when Ventura returns from the wars."[28] The third part, of course, does not belong to the village tale originally told to Fernán Caballero, and has probably two sources: the history, verified and legendary, of Diego Corrientes, which appealed to a sense of the local color, ideally Spanish, and didactic; and the Romantic interest in this stock character. Here, then, is the strength of Fernán Caballero illustrated most convincingly through the fortune of being able to trace the development of *The Family of Alvareda* in that the qualities of observation, realism, and a story basis in fact have resulted in the first two parts of the novel as an innovative, contemporary, and revealing vignette of regional life in Andalucía. Likewise, the weakness of Fernán Caballero is too apparent in the third part when, by dint of artistic uncertainty or the desire to reinforce the defense of the past and the moral, religious values she cherished so sincerely, the reliance is placed on the current Romantic techniques and a repetitive sermonizing, together with a call to an emotional, sentimental, and melodramatic catharsis, again in accord with Romanticism.

Apparently, twenty years passed between the narration, notes, and draft, and the publication as a feuilleton in *El Heraldo*; or, at least, no mention appears of the embryonic manuscript in any correspondence, a barren period, anyway, for epistolary revelations by Fernán Caballero. Despite her somewhat cantankerous comments about editorial vagaries, which often seemed to have effected advantageous changes in her works, the proof about the efficacy of a revision for the *El Heraldo* serialization is seen in the fact that "there are only two radical differences between the *Heraldo* version and that of the standard text of the *Obras completas* and these are both found in the third part of the novel."[29] Again, this third part becomes the focus for alterations; but the changes are perhaps not without significance for the understanding of Fernán Caballero's art and philosophy. In

the newspaper, the seventh chapter of the third part is shorter
by the omission thereby of the descriptive paeans to the symbolism of the church, certainly a Romantic and very recurrent,
subjective obsession with the author; but *El Heraldo* includes
in this chapter an explanation about the fate of the treacherous
"El Presidiario," who is converted into a Judas figure by his
shame, flight, and suicide after betraying Diego. Curiously, the
first change, by a more concise, impartial narration, strengthens
the novel; and the second change pursues too blatantly and
unconvincingly the analogies between Christ and Diego. The
omission in book form of this exaggerated argument is a victory
against Romanticism and for Realism—and for a better novel.
The second change of consequence for the complete works is
the elimination of a long, diversionary scene in Sevilla where
an Englishman and a Frenchman are conversing inanely and
are thereby the butt for Fernán Caballero's antipathy and prej-
udices about foreigners (with a few, derogatory remarks added
about Germans, also). Good taste and sound literary judgment
have happily discarded this episode without any loss to the
structure and ideas of *The Family of Alvareda.*

The minor changes, nevertheless, provide insights into the
Realistic concepts of Fernán Caballero and her strong opinions
about morality; and these differences of opinion also demonstrate
the timid, puritanical approach to Realism, still a noteworthy
advance from the ethereal treatments of the Romantics. For
example, the discovery of Ventura and Rita in the stable is
described in the final version very generally: "What a two-
edged dagger for Ana, the honorable woman, the loving mother.
Ventura was close to Rita" (I, 174). In the newspaper, *El Heraldo,* the scene is more specifically mentioned: "What a two-
edged dagger for Ana, the honorable woman, the loving mother.
Ventura and Rita were frolicking in that withdrawn and hidden
place." Finally, the edition by 1856 had been altered to read:
"What a two-edged dagger for Ana, the honorable woman, the
loving mother. Ventura and Rita, in that withdrawn and hidden
place, were becoming aroused."[30] The dilemma, consequently,
appears to revolve about the use of an adequate verb—not too
specific, however—to describe the flirtatious conduct of the two
lovers. Undoubtedly, this flirtation with the implication of a
full-fledged affair is as far as the author, editors (and probably

censors of 1849) would permit in a literary work. Another brief illustration of Fernán Caballero's insistence upon a veneer of shy realism is her complaint (in the same letter as mention of the above episode between Ventura and Rita) about the 'unnecessary innovation" of the Duque de Rivas by making one of the main characters, probably Perico, drunk at the time of the attempted sacrilege against the church. Her reasoning is that this additional disparagement went counter to the scene and the character, although she has endeavored to show how the action brings a just punishment on all the culprits and is logical in view of Perico's moral degradation. Perhaps, once more, Fernán Caballero cannot place literature above devotion to the Church; and the use of physical symbols of the ecclesiastical presence (the monastery in *The Sea Gull*, the abandoned church in *The Family of Alvareda*, the characters of Brother Gabriel, the novice Marcela) first leads her away from full-fledged realism and, secondly, often turns her aside into a digressive, dogmatic defense of religion. But the text of the last-named novel, with a few other revisions and corrections, has stood the test of time after the first complete works of 1856; and the only contribution, differing from that edition, came in 1861 with the appendices—not an integral part of the novel.

Whatever may be the position of *The Family of Alvareda* vis-à-vis *The Sea Gull*, the progress of the novel is the best example among Fernán Caballero's achievements of the early development of her art—and the appearance in Spain of Realism. The genesis of the novel reveals how far the author was prepared to advance and to change the genre; and to what extent her ideas and ideology produced a worthwhile story. "Even so unpretentious a piece of literature as *The Family of Alvareda* may undergo all sorts of experiences from its birth as a village anecdote to its maturity as one of the humbler classics," concludes Hespelt. "That it survived its infancy at all is probably due to the interested solicitude of Washington Irving; some of the blemishes of its maturity may be due to its editors; in general its development parallels that of its author, its youthful exuberance and prodigality of material giving way to the disciplined restraint of middle age."[31]

CHAPTER 4

Other Novelistic Achievements

FERNÁN Caballero's popular successes, stimulated by the continuing reception and sales of *The Sea Gull* and *The Family of Alvareda*, revealed the soundness and accuracy of her ideas for the development of a new novel in the second half of the nineteenth century. Next, in *Clemencia* and *Lágrimas*, she produced in the first case the most autobiographical contribution among her works (as well as her longest novel), and in the second book she returned to the place, Villamar, of her surprising triumph in *The Sea Gull*. Both novels take place in the contemporary period and show realistic, psychologically motivated heroines surrounded by an environment and circumstances unfavorable, often hostile, and leading to the destruction of the individual happiness of a woman. Again, the Realism of Fernán Caballero blends compromisingly yet harmoniously with the Romantic inheritance of the past and her family, and of course with the firm (too frequently inflexible) code of traditionalism and Catholic morality. But the foot forward in the direction of feminine individualism—for often the main character in a novel—has been taken; and Fernán Caballero's themes, disguised and mildly rendered, cannot be disregarded that a woman as a person evolves with as much right as her male counterpart in the current, realistic world of mid-century, that a woman is shunted aside in terms of understanding and independence, and that a woman is unable to break through the barrier of enforced humility, obedience, and sacrifice, without becoming liberated, however, in the flashy, bold, and degrading manner of "the free woman." Fernán Caballero prefers an eclectic role for a woman with a strong defense, nevertheless, of traditional, idealistic qualities but with this humble request for recognition of some individuality.

I Clemencia

Again in her prologues, Fernán Caballero supplies a revealing, charming, and whimsical approach to her works; and she even writes as an aside that "I always read the prefaces, dear reader, for at times they are the best part of the work" (II, 8). More seriously, Fernán Caballero shows herself aware of the impor- tance and distinctions among her heroines: "What I show you in this novel is the life of a woman, with simple and daily happen- ings as are found in every woman's life and are indispensable in every novel. Clemencia, as contrasted with Lágrimas, who is the type of the sad, weak, and abandoned woman, is the type of the exuberant, cheerful, and happy woman. It is more difficult to make her interesting! I hope to succeed in making her pleas- ant!" (II, 9). There is, then, the sure literary endeavor to develop a certain character—and also to explain the attempt to the reading public and critics.

Clemencia, of course, must be read critically also as a running autobiography on Fernán Caballero's life, an interpretation which apparently eluded her contemporaries and still contains room for further clarification.[1] The novel, then, is more than one additional contribution to Fernán Caballero's Realism: *Clemencia* stands out as an example of the confessional literature, popularized by the Romantics in all countries, and as a frank, honest, psy- chological study of an individual woman. *Clemencia,* before any currents in the novel of introspective, unique, and fascinating characterizations, provides glimpses into the dilemmas posed to a woman by the rigidities (and mounting challenges) of the nineteenth-century Spanish social system. "Anyone who has read the magnificent pages of *Clemencia,* that confession and passion- ate apology that Cecilia made for herself," concludes Herrero, "can see how that thread which stitches the memories and notes of another time is, at times, an inspiration that can produce some of the most beautiful works of the past century."[2]

The threads of the plot, therefore, are traced more easily—and revealingly—through keeping in mind the biographical facts where, however, Fernán Caballero once again plays the game of skillfully concealing her identity. Her novelistic theories, nevertheless, are exposed immediately, and she has no qualms about stating directly her theses by selecting at the very begin- ning a quotation from each of three authors, David, Valon, and Balzac ("the profound Balzac" as she calls him typically in the several references in *Clemencia* to her favorite French author), in order to indicate psychology, observation, and ideas, respectively, as the aims of this book. She illustrates these points, for example, by indicating in *Clemencia* at the end of the seventh chapter in the first part (again there are the favorite three parts for a novel in this work): "What happens in this chapter is an exact outline of social life, such as we have made it; this is to say, a fusion of games and frivolous laughter, which are displayed, and of passions and profound sorrows, which are hidden" (II, 36). This insistence upon exactness also extended to the technical matters of publication when she wrote to Hartzenbusch about the advantages of *Clemencia* to appear first as a book rather than as serialization, primarily, according to her view, to reduce the number of printing errors.[3] But her remarks about the length of the novel (with some fears that the editor's and censor's scissors might cut excerpts without her knowledge) also unveil her paradoxical wish for obscurity because Fernán Caballero wanted the novel to be published quickly and integrally, with no mention of any possible repercussions, personally and socially. *Clemencia*, which Herrero follows very closely in his interpretation of Fernán Caballero's life,[4] is in fact the only work in which the author is so intrusive—to excellent advantage—and provides such a brilliant self-portrait.

Clemencia introduces the heroine, an orphan of sixteen, into the home of her aunt, the Marquesa de Cortegana, whose two daughters, Constancia, nineteen, and Alegría, seventeen, are by their personalities the antitheses of the innocent, modest, kind and naive Clemencia (a very complimentary portrait of the author by herself). Clemencia's aunt, in order to get rid of possible competition for her daughter in the hope of winning the Marqués de Valdemar, accepts the offer of marriage for her niece with Fernando Guevara, an army captain, who has made a cruel bet with his equally dissolute companions that, after only a first glimpse of Clemencia Ponce, he can win the girl as a bride within one week. The marriage is a disaster: Fernando mocks Clemencia for her virtues, passiveness, and humility and the girl, on the verge of a nervous and physical breakdown, finds security only in religion and the code of obedience, taught to her as a child. The revelations about "this incompatibility of natures," as Fernán Caballero discreetly defines the marital conflict, nevertheless add a considerably advanced dimension to the modern Spanish novel and certainly place *Clemencia* as a Realistic novel, firmly and securely.[5] For example, Fernando, bringing home a print of Venus caressing Adonis, coarsely makes fun of the embarrassed innocence of Clemencia and insults her for being an inexperienced product of convent school education. Fernán Caballero, defending Clemencia (and rather clearly in this tragedy her own disastrous first marriage), attacks strongly and bitterly one of her bugbears, the free woman, as previously exemplified sadly in Marisalada and Rita: "This terrible life at the side of a man, whom only the word, atrocious, defines well, a worthy husband for a young girl from those emancipated ones who say with a candid cynicism that they want lovers or husbands who surpass them in audacity and energy" (II, 43). Indeed, all the brief glimpses into the psychological difficulties of the couple, although of course sympathy is with Clemencia as essentially the wronged person in the marriage, are disturbingly accurate about the condition of young girls, who in Spain at this time, were forced into marital unions without their consent—as Moratín in *El sí de las niñas* (*When a Girl Says Yes*) had earlier criticized in his play of 1806. Fernán Caballero, by 1852 in *Clemencia*, could then contribute a personal note to this social problem and, whether unwittingly or not, she is demonstrating that the ignorance of young girls about the sexual aspects of marriage is often fatal to a happy union. Of course, there is no mention, directly, of the sexual problem in the marriage between Fernando and Clemencia, and of course the former is an insensitive, sadistic individual; but the implications are abundant that Clemencia's ignorance is some source of the trouble. At any rate, Clemencia, like Fernán Caballero, is given release by the sudden death of her husband, shortly after the marriage. The unhappy widow, suffering from feelings of guilt, is sent with Constancia to the country by the Marquesa de Cortegana because Constancia (the main concern for the marquesa rather than Clemencia) has fallen in love with a young officer of whom her mother disapproves. Another of Fernán Caballero's techniques from Romanticism, a terrible storm, ends also melodramatically (and Romantically) the first part with Constancia's discovery of the young officer's corpse, washed ashore after the hurricane.

Clemencia goes to the country to live with her deceased husband's father, Martín de Guevara, and his brother, an abbot, with whom she studies philosophy, literature, and art. Don

Martín's nephew, Pablo Guevara, falls in love with Clemencia,
but she cannot accept him as a suitor or a husband: "Clemencia,
on her part, only loved Pablo as a brother. She was still very
girlish, and she lacked experience in knowing her cousin's worth"
(II, 67). After rescuing Clemencia from an attack by a wild
bull and receiving her gratitude in the words, "You have given
me more than life; you have delivered me from the most frightful
of deaths" (II, 76), Pablo is rewarded by Don Martín with the
permission to marry Clemencia. And Don Martín endeavors to
persuade Clemencia to accept his nephew—another example of
the familiar coercion (in this case gentle and respectful) exerted
on girls to accept marriages favorable to Benavente's later-
expressed *intereses creados* ("vested interests"). At stake for Don
Martín is the *mayorazgo* (entailed estate), which he wants to
see assured before his death. Clemencia rejects Don Martín's
suggestion about accepting Pablo, and after the former's death
(followed by the abbot's demise), Clemencia and Pablo decide to
go separate ways, she to live in Sevilla and he to remain on the
estate. Pablo, in fact, refuses to marry Clemencia, although he
might have won her hand because of her moral feelings toward
Don Martín's request, for "if Pablo had had more worldly knowledge, he would have known how to take advantage of those
beautiful moments of compassion to win for himself a heart which
beat with admiration and gratitude, subjugated now by the
noble means which subjugate noble souls; but his timidity
paralyzed him, his modesty discouraged him, and his scrupulous-
ness stopped him" (II, 104).

In Sevilla, Clemencia (like Marisalada in the big, bad city)
is susceptible to the flatteries of the polite, hypocritical *tertulias*
where she meets at one of these social gatherings, the Viscount
Carlos de Brian, a Frenchman, and Sir George Percy, an Englishman, who represent snobbish, wealthy noblemen (and foreigners,
another featured target of Fernán Caballero's aversions). However, Clemencia falls in love with Percy who, unknown to her,
has confidently predicted that he can break down the moral
resistance of this proud, honorable Spanish woman—a more
sophisticated version of her first husband's boast and bet. And,
in fact, Clemencia almost succumbs to the Englishman's charms
and appealing dialogue; but religion, in the background of the
young widow's feelings, slowly restrains her from yielding to

temptation and eventually causes the truth about Percy to become evident to her, as in this instance:

> Yes! Sir George is the type of man who has abjured and broken all relationship with the past, and who, proceeding without a beacon toward the unknown, follows a path that he proclaims as true and that he does not know where it leads him.
>
> So it was that the immense distance which separated their souls, and which each day seemed to her to expand, opened today before Clemencia like an abyss; but her love for Sir George was too intense for her to retreat easily: that fatal man was her first love; her tears were shed on the inside, ardent and corrosive.[6]

The whole setting, and especially this description of Clemencia, are very evidently Romantic, although of course the familiar drawing rooms (as in *The Sea Gull*) supply realistic, *costumbrista* surroundings, drawn again from Fernán Caballero's observations and memories as the Marquesa de Arco-Hermoso. And again, to solve the developing plot complications, so Romantic and moralistic, Fernán Caballero turns toward a realistic solution, in keeping with her ideological orientations, however. Clemencia's rejection of Percy is more profoundly the refusal to accept the nineteenth-century currents of positivism, irreverence, cynicism, and amorality (according to Fernán Caballero). Clemencia and Percy symbolize two worlds: she is the representative of the past, holding to the ideals and virtues disappearing quickly and sadly; he is the modern man—and the symbol of the victorious future, unfortunately for the author—who will also destroy all vestiges of the idealized, sentimentalized traditions. Nevertheless, in this novel Fernán Caballero does not admit defeat, ending her story with an exemplary thesis of the superiority of the past. Clemencia returns to the country estate, where she spent so many happy fruitful years (eight to be exact) in the second part; and she marries Pablo, whom she recognizes as the guardian of moral, religious, and traditional qualities, admitting to herself humbly that she was led by emotional factors rather than by logical analysis to reject him previously as a model husband. Together, they will care for the *mayorazgo* (preserving thereby the past), become the center of a small, influential society by dint of their good example as a happy, married couple; and, in short, become an island of virtue and tradition, lashed by the stormy seas of outside events, however, as Clemencia and Pablo are aware from

visitors' remarks about the attacks of foreigners—and Spaniards—
on their way of life. Of course, this conclusion is idealistic and
sentimental; but Fernán Caballero has attempted to shift from a
Romantic to a Realistic attitude in her heroine, from passion to
love, from foreign lover to native husband, from the city to the
country, and from the new to the old. These traits, while not
limited to the novel of Realism, are found in some degree in later
works of her successors, such as Pereda, Alarcón, and Palacio
Valdés, that is to say, in the regional, local color novel. But
Clemencia's choice between Percy and Pablo is certainly motivated logically and successfully, and perhaps the evident sources
in her own life enabled Fernán Caballero to depict with this
verisimilitude an advanced psychological portrait of a woman,
trapped by very human and normal instincts.

The novel, nevertheless, lacks in the admittedly realistic
and natural dialogue a contemporary interest for the present
reader, which may be a compensatory explanation for the
popularity of Fernán Caballero's novel in her own generation.
For example, the discussions in the drawing rooms only once
bring up one of the important topics of The Sea Gull, the modern
novel. Clemencia, on this single occasion, insists that a moral
aim or object is essential in the novel, more so in the spirit than
in the words, "as the English generally practice it."[7] Style, in
fact, whether it be the individual expression of the writer or the
correct usage of the language, may indeed be no more than a
minor aspect of the novel; and Clemencia even states that an
erudite, flowery vocabulary, without a corresponding naturalness and sincerity, detracts from the interest and acceptance of
audiences.[8] Although much, perhaps most, of Clemencia is
authentic in terms of autobiography (as continuing criticism
has confirmed), the literary biography still contains problems
and is a mine for future raw materials about Fernán Caballero.
Thus, the traumatic escape from the wild bull, if a true vignette
from the author's experiences, may be explanatory, at least in part,
for her pronounced antipathies against bullfighting in The Sea
Gull and the appendices to The Family of Alvareda.[9]

II Lágrimas

Lágrimas, just as Clemencia, is the given name of the protagonist of the novel of the title, and hence will not be translated

to its common-noun meaning, "Tears." With *Lágrimas*, the success of *The Sea Gull* is hopefully to be repeated by a return to Villamar; but the book aroused later much criticism for Fernán Caballero's political interventions, accusations which she denied as inaccurate interpretations of the novel. However, these refutations of any attacks against democratic partisans and political parties during the composition of *Lágrimas* should be balanced against the facts that she prepared the novel in 1848, certainly a revolutionary period against conservatism and traditionalism, and that she called the book *Lágrimas o la España actual. (Lágrimas or Present Spain)*.[10] Internal evidence from the plot, characters, and usual sermonizing in *Lágrimas* demonstrates a very harsh, bitter picture of what the nineteenth century has brought to rural Spain in particular, as was indicated earlier in our critical analysis of *The Sea Gull*.

"More than happenings, we paint events," Fernán Caballero states in an early chapter of this *novela de costumbres contemporáneas* (novel of contemporary customs), "more than heroes of a novel, we trace true portraits of real life" (II, 122). Although the characters of Momo, Don Modesto, and Mystical Rose appear as minor characters in *Lágrimas*, they have basically no great role to play in the new civilization of the nineteenth century, *el siglo de las luces* ("the century of enlightenment"). Finally, and surprisingly, the retiring author shows that she is really not so shy by mentioning herself after a charming, humorous explanation of the delicate art of flirtation by a suitor's taking in his hands the fan of a girl: "You will know in the course of your life the advantages and some day you will say: 'Blessed be Fernán Caballero, whom I know but to serve her'" (II, 163). Another major difference—and advance in the Realistic novel— is Fernán Caballero's more accurate rendition of dialect, both the Andalusian speech patterns and the Galician linguistic phenomena; and these adherences to the language characteristics possess a structural role in the novel because they are consistently employed humorously to indicate the comical features of the personages.

What is the cause for the vast alterations taking place in Villamar, that microcosm of Spain? Fernán Caballero repeats throughout *Lágrimas* the phrase *la noble ambición* ("noble ambition"), to signify the transfer from a natural aristocracy (she is careful not to accept an aristocracy of birth as the preferred class) to a financial aristocracy. Money is the basis of this new social class, and the great man of the nineteenth century is the millionaire, whom she scornfully describes in one chapter with a series of paragraphs beginning with the words, *El millonario* (II, 150-51). And the worst specimen is the miser, for whom she may have found antecedents in Molière's Harpagon (she mentions "the great Molière" in the novel), in Balzac (mentioned of course on more than one occasion for his similar criticisms of the nineteenth century), and at least some affinities in Dickens. Logically, then, the villain (and the designation refers without doubt to a character, usually not so classified in Fernán Caballero's novels) is Don Roque la Piedra, a millionaire with the appropriate surname meaning "the rock." He is villainous from the first chapter when his wife dies during a storm at sea and he callously ignores her pleas for compassion toward their child, Lágrimas, by thinking rather of the dowry for himself and the economies effected by a burial at sea; and his villainies continue in the last chapter when, despite the dying pleas of Lágrimas to forgive the debts of the Marquesa de Alocaz, Don Roque la Piedra lies and plans to collect the money. His child's death makes no impression on the heartless father, and in a week, he is busily engaged in business deals once again; and Lágrimas, her clothes, the bed, and furniture from the room burned because of her consumptive disease, vanishes: "Nothing remained of her, not even the memory!" (II, 232). This vision of the social reality of the nineteenth century, bitter and unrelentingly depressing, leads to the reaction of advocates of the age against Fernán Caballero; and the impact upon the author may have been equally devastating (perhaps unconsciously) because she failed to continue in the same mode: "The end, extremely pessimistic, reflects faithfully the vision of the author with respect to the mesocratic society of her epoch, a vision that explains the fact that the novelist withdraws from the probings into the reality of the epoch and takes refuge, more and more, in the idyllic vision of her local color sketches and her stories of pious type where she better finds herself as a writer."[11]

It is ironic, then, that at the precise moment when Fernán Caballero has written a novel so attuned to the age and so much in advance of Galdós, she immediately turned aside from this harsh—but so accurate in many unfortunate and unhappy ways—vision to her illusions, her dreams about a Spain that never existed in general terms, but existed in small particulars for her joyful years as the Marquesa de Arco-Hermoso. For example, she shifted in *Lágrimas* from her positive qualities of observation about landscapes to character sketches:

A *costumbrismo* more of types than of landscapes is the one developed in *Lágrimas*. In this and in many other things, she places herself at a distance from *The Sea Gull*; if indeed the protagonist is a woman, she is much sweeter, more resigned; we could say that she is a heroine of her silences. Perhaps the ground is the same and the landscape identical, only that they are kept at a distance in order to emphasize the daughter of the tropics, placed and involved with an overseas legend, a kind of wild violet, according to one critic. The types of Galdosian stock stand out: Don Roque la Piedra, Don Jeremías Tembleque, Don Perfecto Cívico, Don Trifón Rubicundo. . . . Why this play of words so frequently in Fernán Caballero? Is it possibly an act of defining through eagerness, something as if to look for qualities of the subject in the expression? Is it possibly an initiation of descriptions, perhaps an eagerness for small syntheses? Perhaps at bottom it was only to follow the historical criterion in order to carry in future evolutions the Spanish novel to the naturalism of Galdós, that is to say, to establish a bridge from the world of Balzac and Dickens to the author of *Misericordia* (*Mercy*), with which the summit and the evolution of the Spanish novelistic art can be considered as having reached. (I, cxxiv-cxxv)

Already, in *Clemencia*, Fernán Caballero had started to paint (her precise word on various occasions for the written observations) these Realistic, almost Naturalistic, characterizations, as for Don Galo Pando, whom she particularly recommends as *mi muy querido* Don Galo Pando ("My very dear Don Galo Pando") in an introductory note to that novel. More specifically, Don Roque la Piedra is the prototype for the Torquemada of Galdós—although direct evidence is lacking despite the knowledge of Fernán Caballero's works by her successor (and master) in the novel of Realism—and the same, self-centered, monetary considerations are uppermost in the schemes of both protagonists. How to make a deal, how to turn a profit, and how to avoid spending money even for the minimum necessities of life are common traits of the two wealthy misers. Of course, the Torquemada of Galdós evolves into a more profoundly fascinating investigation of the conflict between materialistic aims and nebulous idealism, and the character strides through four novels of the *Torquemada* series. But Fernán Caballero's one impressive venture into the new, frightening world of the nineteenth century brings her abreast of Galdós, before she shrinks back to safety in the *costumbrista* escapism, founded on observations and narrations.

Don Roque la Piedra, dominating the main thread of the action, nevertheless fails in several instances to advance significantly in his quest for wealth, power, social position, and political advantage. The apparent success of this man of the nineteenth century, as Fernán Caballero so determinedly creates him, must be painted finally as a form of defeat, keeping in mind the author's ideology and constant preaching. Her scorn, indeed, extends to the whole age, which spawns such creatures, as in this vivid thrust at Don Roque:

> The type whom we are going to delineate is that one who, having left the dust of bad places, without education, without honor and even without shame (this last bond through which a man belongs to society), without more God than greed, nor more ambition than that of hoarding, freely giving over his good name, dignity, alien opinion, without paying attention to means, arrives at the apogee of wealth through low, illicit, and criminal means. This odious being who combines admirably the vices of both classes, those of the poor and those of the rich, is a plague coming from the dregs of revolutions, or else from the confusion of ideas and delights of civil wars, or else from the chaos of disorders or mysteries of the wandering impunity in all countries, and which flees from contempt with fearful brow, preserved against reprobation with its golden shield. (II, 150)

Fernán Caballero's use of the familiar characters from *The Sea Gull*, with direct references to their traits (usually good except for Momo, of course) and with remarks about Stein for his humanitarianism in Villamar, is only a link, however, between the two novels. The author has skillfully and with outstanding contemporary relevance utilized the monastery as the symbol for the changing worlds of the two novels, *The Sea Gull* and *Lágrimas*. One may certainly recall at this point the poetic, sentimental, introspective reactions of Stein as he first saw the ecclesiastical building and as he later described the edifice more fully; and indeed Fernán Caballero starts this very significant passage with that beautiful recollection from *The Sea Gull*:

> The visit which these men of speculation and money made to the monastery was not like the one that Stein, the German doctor, had made with Brother Gabriel. No, no! These men only looked at the cover of that magnificent book, without paying attention to the fact that the leaves and the contents of them were missing; because they did not understand this, they only looked at the rose staff, the height, the bells of that proud piano, without noting that the strings were missing and, consequently, the sound and the harmony. They would not have heard it, and thus they did not miss it. (II, 207)

The contrast is decidedly effective, and the poetic imagery in accord with the previous descriptions. But Fernán Caballero, again in contact with a physical symbol of religion, falls into the trap, literary and aesthetic, of allowing her ideas to interfere with the artistic process; and she launches into an increasingly strident rebuttal of the age which permits such changes. Her error, ironically, is that she forgets the story, the characters, and the particular episode; and her arguments lose their force and persuasiveness by their fanatical presentation:

> Seated upon the sumptuous stone steps of the high altar they discussed how to degrade sooner that portentous work of the piety of ancestors and to wrench from it the only thing remaining thereto: the austere majesty of solitude, the profound melancholy of abandonment.
>
> Oh my God! . . . If there is someone who can blame us for raising our weak voice, shouting your own words, "Give to God that which is God's and to Caesar that which is Caesar's," place the blame on us, it is all right. What does praise or criticism signify for an obscure and unknown being to cut short on his lips the words of truth, the buds from his heart? What right do you have to destroy what others built? Do you believe that you can speak to the feelings of the fervent until you, like God to the waves of the sea, arrive at such a point? If the present generation condemns in their works the generation which built them, the day will come in which the future generation may condemn with quite more reason the ruins which this generation caused. Cut out the gangrene before it causes more damage and let it be said that if it is for wise men to err, it is for noble men to recognize the error and to correct it. (II, 207)

However, Fernán Caballero next returns to a more tranquil, artistic, and convincing manner to attack this antipathetical event of modern times with the aid of an old literary ally, Momo. Aunt María's brutish grandson again proves his importance for conveying winningly (for the ideas, if not for his personality) whatever is desired at this stage. And, in fact, Momo makes the best commentary on the two businessmen's stinginess by his mockery of their less than generous tip for his work as a guide to the monastery. The physiology of Momo (the Balzacian ideas are again expressed on various occasions in *Lágrimas*) shows that Fernán Caballero recognized, at least partially, the value of this character, as was mentioned in our critical analysis of *The Sea Gull*, although she unfortunately did not exploit enough the possibilities of Momo's role.

The humiliating end of the monastery is then explained in brief, incisive fashion:

One proposed turning the monastery into a paper factory, and the lack of water made him abandon the project. The other spoke of a tanning factory; Momo, who was consulted, answered with disagreeable reasons that they would have to bring the skins from Cádiz since thereabouts only billy goats in the summer and hogs in the winter were killed. Finally, Don Roque judged that the most lucrative thing would be to demolish the edifice and to sell the materials, as had been done with other buildings; but Momo said that there was no one there who would buy such rich materials, even if they were undersold, because there was no way to use them.

Then, the men headed back after Don Roque majestically gave two *reales* to Momo, who was on the point of throwing them at their feet. (II, 207)

Anyone in agreement with Fernán Caballero's defense of the old life in Villamar has to give approval to Momo's reaction, correct as in *The Sea Gull* through his very obstreperousness, but this time more overt, and directly committed to higher motives against the encroaching materialism of the nineteenth century. The two entrepreneurs are Don Roque and Don Perfecto Cívico, the mayor of Villamar; their unsavory alliance constitutes the main thrust of the novel's plot, at least in the second half. At the beginning of *Lágrimas*, which Fernán Caballero has described in a subtitle as a *novela de costumbres contemporáneas* ("novel of contemporary customs"), the contemporary problem is immediately advanced after the initial Romantic scene of the death of Don Roque's wife and the pathetic introduction of Lágrimas. Don Roque la Piedra and Don Jeremías Tembleque climbed the financial ladder of success through a stroke of good luck and also through "overcoming obstacles by pushing hard" (II, 111), being joined finally by another hustling individual, Don Trifón Rubicundo. This trio is not devoid of some ironic humor on Fernán Caballero's part: she has them refer sanctimoniously to the *malditos yanquis* ("cursed Yankees") and *malditos norteamericanos* ("cursed Americans") because of these foreigners' undue emphasis upon money during their own discussions about finances; and she keeps designating the three plotters by the honorific "Don." After Tembleque's sudden death, caused by a seizure upon reading that the revolution of 1848 in Paris has wiped out all his funds in that capital (an understated description of effective poetic justice by the author), Don Roque gravitates toward the mayor of Villamar as a business crony.

This depressing history of the monetary maneuvers of the new "financial aristocracy" is relieved, however, by the entrance into the action of three *señoritos* (playboys), Marcial, Fabián, Jenaro, who, again with a delicately contrived poetic justice, squander the money, so precious to their families, and lead idle lives of pleasure and some literary discussions (the only brief return in *Lágrimas* to the frequently enlightened *tertulias* in *The Sea Gull*). All these diverse groups merge in terms of this complex plot of *Lágrimas* when the Marquesa de Alocaz, after opposing the marriage of her daughter, Reina, to Jenaro, gives her permission, convinced in large part by Don Roque's obnoxious behavior. The latter, coming to collect the money borrowed from him by the Marquesa de Alocaz, proposes marriage to the stunned noblewoman; and she sells possessions to rid herself of the unwelcome suitor and also to secure the free choice of Reina about a husband, despite Jenaro's disadvantages. The Romantic contribution derives from the tragic fate of Lágrimas: Don Roque's daughter is sincerely loved by the victims of her father, the Marquesa de Alocaz and Reina. Don Roque and Don Perfecto Cívico plan to recoup some of their stakes in the power positions of Villamar by agreeing on the marriage between

Lágrimas and Tiburcio, the mayor's son. But the young man, unable to face a life in the future with Lágrimas, absconds with his father's money, which had been intended to secure the monastery as a factory. Lágrimas, ill and unwanted, dies despite her final pleas to her father, "What can money do against the will of God?" (II, 231).

Undoubtedly, the spur for Fernán Caballero in the events of that critical year of 1848 throughout Europe prompted her to complete this very successful novel—surely *Lágrimas* falls within this category despite the author's disclaimer of being the writer of "novels"—and, including the ideology of a love for the past and the stable, and the frequent outbursts against the nineteenth century, she still lifted literature above person, above orientations. Certainly, her art reached a high level of interpreting the present times: her use of the word "contemporary" as a part of her descriptive title; and the chronological period, from October, 1837, until October, 1848, when the revolutionary upheavals were terminated and the results digested to some degree. The irony, blended with the inherently sarcastic and sardonic, comes to the surface with masterly skill in the last chapters when Don Roque makes his bid for the Marquesa de Alocaz' hand; and his defeat, unrecognized fully by him because of his obdurate ambition, is subtly drawn without, fortunately, Fernán Caballero's persistent intervention. *Lágrimas*, as a title, is of course appealing, particularly for the female audience; but the heroine is uninterestingly presented because of her stereotyped role as the Romantic maiden. Inexplicably, then, Fernán Caballero, determined to oppose the novels of Romanticism, lapsed into the acceptance of this genre, although the contrast between Lágrimas and the "financial aristocracy" of the nineteenth century, especially her father, reinforces her thesis of the evils of the coming age. For example, the letters, inserted toward the novel's end, explain events and broaden the scope of the characterization, but the interest lags because of constant epistolary references instead of some variety with direct action. However, the artistry within the entire novel compensates for this last aesthetic decline, again having as an explanation the probable wrath of Fernán Caballero against the reports about 1848. "We find a good example of this double focus, poetic or satiric, which the author uses to describe Spanish social reality," states Fuentes, "by contrasting *The Sea*

Gull with *Lágrimas,* a novel written later, and in part as a continuation, but with a diametrically opposite intention: the first novel contains a poetical exaltation of the traditional social order, while the second, significantly subtitled 'Present Spain,' contains a biting satire of the liberal society."[12]

III *Two Novels on the Polarization*

It is clear that Fernán Caballero wrote various works some time before they were published; and only the degree of completion, together with some possible alterations because of editorial advice, especially that of Hartzenbusch, seems to be the moot point about this technical question. It is likewise clear that Fernán Caballero drew her material principally from her early years, approximately, as the Marquesa de Arco-Hermoso. Or, at least, her favorite decade was, curiously enough, the period of saddest political liberties for Spain—depending of course upon the individual's affiliations. This era, embracing in general 1820-1830, is the historical moment for the very distinct majority of Fernán Caballero's writings, although important endeavors, such as *The Sea Gull* and *Lágrimas,* utilize that critical year, 1848. If Fernán Caballero can timidly glance at the coming world in the second half of the nineteenth century, retreating quickly as is evident in her major books, she can also look backward, with less fear and more objectivity, at least from the memories of her own happy years as the Marquesa de Arco-Hermoso. In this contribution to the historical novel, if the criterion of the nineteenth century rather than a remote, exotic past as in the Romantic influence of that Spanish favorite, Scott, is accepted as the time, Fernán Caballero has foreshadowed briefly and mildly the Galdosian mastery of this genre in the *Episodios nacionales* (*National Episodes*) after his first efforts in *La fontana de oro* (*The Golden Fountain*) and *El audaz* (*The Bold One*) where he, coincidentally, utilizes the same political setting as in her two novels. These two novels, *Elia, o La España treinta años ha* (*Elia or Spain Thirty Years Ago*) and *Un servilón y un liberalito o tres almas de Dios* (*A Loyalist and a Liberal or Three Souls of God*), portray basically the same Spanish problem: the intensifying polarization of the nation into liberal and traditionalist camps.[13] Although Fernán Caballero's sympathies, of course, are seen completely allied with the defenders of the monarchy, established religion, and the present social system, nevertheless she has probed deeply and correctly into the consequences of this ideological split in the national life. Spain is heading toward a civil war in which brother will fight against brother—as in *Elia*—and friendships will be broken or impossible to maintain, as in the second novel. Of course, Fernán Caballero is not impartial in her depictions because her liberal, progressive (radical, for her) characters are less agreeable as persons, outspoken in their views to a point of discourtesy, callous about the conservative beliefs, and altogether too erratic for any role in the political governance of the state.

All in all, Fernán Caballero's ideals, while pronounced directly and repeatedly, do not detract from a contemporary interest in the two novels, although the fact that these stories are not as long as the four books analyzed up to now may be a technical remedy for her temptations to compose digressive, prolix, and harsh rebuttals to her whipping boys of the nineteenth century. However, the plots are in essence carefully constructed, the dialogues are lively and realistic, and the characters drawn with verisimilitude. But the main value is perhaps in this prophetic vision of the Spanish future, which explains in part the tragic endings of both novels. There is no doubt that Fernán Caballero, throughout her life, was more than a Romantic, enamored of the Spanish heritage, such as Washington Irving; she was a sincere lover of all facets of her Spanish background, a cause for her strongly-worded defense of Spain. She, like Galdós, and certainly some of the men of the Generation of 1898, grasped fully the implications of the ideological polarization of Spain; and Fernán Caballero tried to express this smoldering tragedy in very personal terms, in the unhappy fates of literary personages. A feature of Fernán Caballero's presentation is the conservative argument that present circumstances (which she approves so wholeheartedly in any case) are preferable to the strife, moral and physical, attendant upon efforts at political and social changes and reforms. It is better, then, to accept the present than to seek the future, that dreadful ogre for Fernán Caballero.

Nevertheless, in her frequent device of "a word from the author to the reader" of *Elia,* Fernán Caballero stresses another thesis: the depiction of a woman who, in opposition to Rousseau's

Héloïse, does not behave sentimentally and melodramatically but rather in an exemplary, rational manner—the author's indirect definition of the application of traditionalist codes to a realistic feminine portrait in the nineteenth century. Her other aims in this novel, in addition to "that delicate feminine modesty," are the familiar purposes of observation, the imitation of nature, and the study of the human heart where, for the last idea, she quotes Balzac, "a profound judge of the human heart" (III, 9-10). The novel opens in 1814 in Sevilla where the *Te Deum*, a Mass of Thanksgiving, is being celebrated for the return of Fernando VII to the Spanish throne after the Napoleonic retreat from the Peninsula; and the Sevillian society is planning to resume a tranquil life with the return of the young men from the War of Independence. Carlos and Fernando Orrea, under the rather domineering control of their mother, are in very evident disagreement about politics: Carlos is liberal, and Fernando is a *servilón*, or a loyalist, a strict defender of the king. However, Fernán Caballero defines quite objectively but sharply these polarized views:

"A liberal . . . is one who wants to destroy the throne with the rights of the crown, the one who wants to destroy religion with the convents, the nobility with their estates, Spain with the imitation of everything English and French, the laws of nature, wanting all of us to be equal. Confound them all!"

"No . . . you are prejudiced, mistaken, badly predisposed. A liberal is one who wants the advancements of the century, and not to fall asleep over the past glories; you are badly informed if you believe any other thing. We true liberals never recognize another government but the one at whose head is the king, and who only professes and approves the Catholic religion." (III, 17)

Carlos falls in love with Elia, another gentle, kind, and submissive heroine of Fernán Caballero's literary women; and the political argument is transferred to the personal level because Fernando opposes his brother's wish to marry Elia, in addition to the enraged refusal of the mother of Carlos. Elia, in the eyes of Fernando, obedient to the established rules of society and his mother, is of a lower social class; and the problem is compounded when Elia's father is revealed to have been a bandit, with her consequent illegitimacy the ultimate in barriers for the Orrea family. However, Elia is also found to be the heir of a consider-

able fortune; and Carlos gets involved in a duel with gossipers
who remark upon the financial motives for his amorous interest
in Elia. The king, opposed to duels, banishes Carlos; and Elia
enters a convent to devote the rest of her life to the Church as
a nun. Carlos returns and fails to persuade Elia to leave her
religious exile to marry him in a very dramatic—and Romantic—
scene. Later, the two brothers, "victims of the terrible and
horrible civil war, the most frightful scourge that man forges
by his own hand" (III, 94), die in battle on opposing sides; Fernando is killed in 1822, defending the king, and Carlos perishes
in 1823, fighting for the lost, liberal cause. Their mother dies
shortly thereafter, mainly of a broken heart because Fernando
would have been a model heir for the family name and Carlos
was the first member of this family, fighting against the cause
of the monarchy and tradition. Esperanza, her daughter, sur-
vives the loss of her mother and brothers; but her two sons die
later in the intermittent but intensifying civil wars and national
chaos of the disastrous nineteenth century in Spain.[14]

A *Loyalist and a Liberal* starts in the year 1823, when the
action of *Elia* terminates; but there is no intended connection,
at least verifiable, between the two stories.[15] There is also a very
noticeable difference in these *novelas cortas* (*short novels*) from
several viewpoints. *Elia*, for instance, is much longer than *A
Loyalist and a Liberal*; and, in fact, the latter would really be
within the genre of the short story. *Elia* has more space thereby
for the illuminating contemporary and personal discussions
about diverse topics, such as celibacy for the clergy (astonishing news for the Spanish about this permission in the Church
of England), a few adverse comments about *Don Quijote* (Cervantes is surprisingly not a favorite with Fernán Caballero), and
the seemingly ubiquitous disparagements of foreigners, their
ways, and especially their influence. Also, the characterization
is broader in *Elia* because of the larger number of personages
and the various, additional episodes.

The subtitle of *tres almas de Dios* in *A Loyalist* . . . refers to
the three residents of the castle of Menesteo who are also
the loyalists in the story: Don José Mentor, the schoolmaster,
his wife, Doña Escolástica, and his sister, Doña Liberata. This
subtitle (and the subsequent refutation of the usual derogatory
nature of the phrase) is explained thus:

This enviable state of soul of theirs, this complete submission and confidence in God, creates gentleness; and this banishes anguished cares, the excesses of sensitivity, the bitterness against men and things. And above all, it creates the beautiful gift of conformity, which spontaneously sprouts in the souls of those persons and which shelters them with its sweet shadow; without their noting even that the tranquility of their spirit is due to the excellence of their souls and that the humorous epithet of "soul of God," with which the world ridicules them with so much lightness, signifies nothing less than having arrived at the apogee of Christianity. Dumas has said very well that greatness, according to God, is not greatness, according to men. (II, 434)

Here is the common complaint of Fernán Caballero: religious exaltation will move the spiritually empty persons of the nineteenth century for a return to the virtues of their predecessors. In the novel, the example of the "three souls of God" influences the liberal fugitive in later years to a more moderate and appreciative attitude toward the past. The story, nevertheless, is told with a great deal of wit and realism as the author is shifting from her explorations in the previous novels to a linear narrative development, with only glimpses at contemporary problems and issues—perhaps unfortunately for her future literary reputation. The plot, as Fernán Caballero consistently maintains, is uncomplicated, although there are a few turns in the action which give an unexpected, surprising direction to the story's progress. Don Leopoldo Ardaz takes refuge in the castle of Menesteo after his flight from loyalist pursuers during the French invasion of Spain in 1823 to restore Fernando VII as king. The three members of the conservative family welcome him, but they immediately disagree on political matters despite the personal warmth of their daily contacts. Don Leopoldo, in fact, starts most of the quarrels by questioning their beliefs and by baiting his hosts in several ways (singing the rebel hymn of Riego, writing "Codex of the Constitution" in the open book of a saint's statue, etc.) with no real malice intended. Before escaping, Don Leopoldo writes a letter to a friend in which he makes fun of his conservative protectors; and the French colonel, questioning the family about the suspected refugee with the threat of imprisonment for all involved, laughs uproariously upon reading the letter, and departs satisfied that the three are innocent. In 1841, Don Leopoldo, now a general on the side of Isabel II, comes back to the castle where he learns that Don José has died, Doña Liberata is ill, and Doña Escolástica is impoverished; and he also learns that the family never used the money he left after his escape from the French troop of soldiers. Don José believed after the narrow escape from imprisonment by the French officer that Don Leopoldo deliberately wrote and left the mocking letter about his hosts in order to save them; but Don Leopoldo explains in shame that the words were not intended to be deceptive. He now helps the two women and confesses that he has outgrown the callousness of his youth, thanks to their example and counsels, and he warns present-day youth not to repeat his immature errors: "If they are young, remember me and do not despair of them ... for they will return, if they are good, to the flock in whose serene setting the soul is uplifted, the heart is unburdened, and the mind rests.... Pity them! God has withdrawn from them because they have withdrawn from God!" (II, 459).

This last paragraph in *A Loyalist* ... confirms as usual the forceful didactic and ideological purposes of Fernán Caballero, and the short novel would have been a great deal more effective and realistic with the omission of this blatantly overt defense of the loyalist cause, religion, and traditionalism. But the initial encounters of the "three souls of God" and Don Leopoldo, with Fernán Caballero's obvious pleasure at the discomfiture of the French colonel, a foreigner, supply the contemporary historical associations and portray truthfully the conflicts, political, psychological, and social, between the two factions in Spain in 1823. The narrative interest, the attempt at distinct characterizations, especially in the three loyalists, and the unexpected plot developments add to Fernán Caballero's interpretation of the Realistic novel; but the adamant sermonizing and stern moralizing in the unnecessary epilogue, though short, detract seriously from the rapid explanations of the last chapter. Fernán Caballero falls into a repeated trap of a too emphatic denunciation of opposing ideas; and the conversion of Don Leopoldo is unmotivated, being almost miraculous. This is probably the author's pious intention and unsatisfactory literary technique. One of the most enlightening procedures, however, occurs in the first chapter where Fernán Caballero, setting the stage as usual with a long, detailed, favorable view of the castle, compares and contrasts sharply her realistic, objective description with the Romantic employments of castles, especially in the Gothic literature of fantasy and imagination. Of course, Fernán Caballero's gaze at last falls, toward the end of this initial chapter, on the portrait of Fernando VII in the castle, a sure sign of her weighted judgment for the royalist party. Perhaps, in pursuit of this same favoritism for her own cause, Fernán Caballero in the title of *A Loyalist* . . . places unconsciously the word *servilón* before *liberalito*, which she writes in the diminutive form, adding the suffix, *ito*, for a possibly humorous or even derogatory effect.[16]

IV *The Other* "Novelas Cortas"

The problem for Fernán Caballero of a standard definition for her contribution to the novel, mentioned at times in the prologues and on other occasions within the works themselves, has been conveniently solved by the artificial division of what she seemed to consider her important writings as *novelas* and *novelas cortas*.[17] The "novels" are frequently provided with an explanatory, defining subtitle which mentions or refers to the idea of *costumbres*—these "customs" of local color, especially Andalusian, vintage. The "short novels" seem to be quite simply the euphemistic, simplified term for novels of less importance in addition to their reduced length, obviously. But the evidence from her letters, written for the most part after the publication of these *novelas cortas* and certainly after the first drafts of the works, is not always clear and is somewhat contradictory about the problem of definition and classification.[18] "How are these books called that Fernán Caballero writes and publishes? To what literary genre do they belong?" are the two questions posed by Montesinos in his approach to the issues of definition and classification. "In order to understand them, it is necessary to state precisely the terms and, at times, to forget the dialectical disposition of Fernán Caballero's spirit, always battling or on the defensive against something. Those terms, furthermore, are filled with a determined content as a work of circumstances, and their significance, in some cases, is not the same that they could have shortly before or that they will have shortly thereafter."[19]

It may be acceptable, then, and certainly convenient to follow the listing, with reservations, of the available complete works.[20] ¡Pobre Dolores! (Poor Dolores!), with the favorite setting of a small Andalusian town, is a narration of the life of one of Fernán Caballero's typical heroines. This type of heroine, and Spanish feminine ideal, is self-sacrificing, devoted, humble, and, of course, the product of a provincial, i.e., Andalusian background. Dolores symbolizes the victory of traditionalism, the country, and morality. Again, Fernán Caballero's didacticism stands out repeatedly and strongly; the problems of the modern age and personal tragedies can be borne stoically only if the lessons of the past and the bedrock of loyalty to absolutism (political, social, and religious) are followed. The plot, then, is constructed primarily on these principles; and this slow-moving action, because of the minor confrontations, is resolved by a tragic coincidence. Lorenzo and Esteban López, returning from forced military service to their home town of Rota, make a mistake at night by believing that a man with Dolores must be her lover. Lorenzo, enraged, kills the supposed lover of Dolores, whom he wanted to marry; and the dying victim is revealed to be Tomás, the brother of Dolores. Although Esteban is prepared to accept death instead of his brother when the former is apprehended by the authorities, the latter appears for his just punishment. Lorenzo is sentenced to imprisonment in the Mariana Islands, and Dolores cannot consent to marriage with anyone. She devotes the rest of her life to prayer and good works, becoming a model for the community. There are as redeeming features to the novel compelling portraits of local color Andalusian types, such as Don Marcelino Toro, Doña Braulia Toro, and the priest, Nolasco, who, like Brother Gabriel in The Sea Gull, has been expelled from any religious residence by the seizure of ecclesiastical properties by the government. Once again, however, Fernán Caballero, placing the action of Poor Dolores! around 1850, makes a reference, utilizing a contemporary problem structurally within the plot, about the injustices of war, the draft lottery, and the hapless peasants—a solidly Realistic mode:

In a few days an edict was publicly posted. This was a dagger thrust, which wounded all the people, which was going to destroy the happiness of many, to cut many ties, and to pierce deeply the hearts of mothers; this edict announced the drawing.

For the peasant, neither the work he yearns for nor the privations which affect him little nor his many children whom he loves are calamities. The drama in the life of the peasant is the draft, the well-named *contribution of blood*. The hand of the minister who signs the decree giving the order would tremble if he knew about the torrents of bitter tears that it is going to cost, the hearts that it is going to break, and the lives it is going to shatter.

When is God going to will that we see civilization throw itself in the arms of Christianity, its parent, and being united, succeed in having men arm themselves only voluntarily and with the sole end of surrounding the throne for its decorum and justice for its strength! (II, 403)

As usual, Fernán Caballero's poetical, rhetorical exaltation is placed first at the service of monarchy and religion; but even if these traditionalist defenses fail to win support and sympathy, her call for justice, against war, in denunciation of military conscription, and in strong advocacy of the already burdened peasantry evokes respect for this concern; it offers a progressive march beyond the Romantic outlook, toward the Realistic approach, and foreshadows the Naturalistic preoccupations.

La Estrella de Vandalia (*The Star of Vandalia*) resembles structurally *Poor Dolores!* in the slow, unexciting action leading to a climactic moment of tragedy built on coincidence. This "short novel," like the previous example, might be more effective if, in view of the *tempo lento* quality, conversion to a shorter piece, or short story, as Fernán Caballero also developed, had been adopted.[21] Again, the setting is lovingly and with leisure unfolded in the first chapter near the city of Sevilla in Andalucía. And there is the stock character in Fernán Caballero's repertoire of the destitute priest (as in *Poor Dolores!*), victim of the land seizures from the Church between 1836 and 1844, Father Buendía. However, the story, as in *The Sea Gull* and *The Family of Alvareda*, revolves about sex and violence, with a physiological portrait of Raimundo, executed at length and in detail, especially as an example of *el insolente*. In the nineteenth century, at least for Fernán Caballero, "the insolent one" has replaced the hypocrite since the latter has lost any attraction with the disappearance of the good and saintly. The abundance of moral lessons and religious ideals impedes this novel seriously; and again, coincidence solves a dreary recital of the above ideology with the action intensified only in the last chapters. Raimundo, ruined morally beyond redemption after a residence in the city, is insanely jealous of Gracia, "the star of Vandalia," because she will marry Alonso instead of consenting to be his wife. On the eve of Gracia's marriage, Raimundo fatally shoots Alonso; and Gracia enters a convent. Years later, Raimundo, embittered and unhappy still, hears a shot and immediately senses that his son has accidentally found the gun used to slay Alonso, and the weapon has been discharged, killing the youth. Only Gracia knows that divine justice has caused this event in reparation for the crime of Raimundo. There are various weaknesses in the story: an extended period of time, over many years, for a brief, important culminating point; the inexplicable failure to connect immediately Raimundo with the crime after his threats in this small town; and the contrived manner in which a gun, kept for so long with one bullet, will be the instrument of retribution. Surely Raimundo would have disposed of the weapon previously, or at least would have refilled the empty chamber or even would have removed the single unused bullet.

Un verano en Bornos (*A Summer in Bornos*) introduces a decidedly innovative technique for Fernán Caballero in the use of the epistolary form throughout the novel; and some critics have tried to see in the story an influence for Juan Valera's *Pepita Jiménez,* one of the major psychological novels of the nineteenth century.[22] However, the letters in Fernán Caballero's novel, since they come from so many individuals, do not really convey in depth the reactions and impressions of the individual. Also, the problems involved are very familiar and likewise not very profound: two girls slowly find themselves falling in love with two young men; and the story ends happily with the marriage announcements for the four principal correspondents. There are many digressive passages throughout the correspondence; the range of interests is wide, but, once more, too many topics prevent any serious discussion, argument, and resolution of the issues. In addition to an attempt at letters forming the basis for a novel, Fernán Caballero abandons her exemplary peasants in Andalucía for a middle-class environment, with a consequent absence of the folklore omnipresent in the other works.

Una en otra (*One in Another*) utilizes the same basic idea of an exchange of letters, but Fernán Caballero is more successful

with this effort because she blends with a great deal of skill
almost two separate stories, creating a rudimentary foreshadowing of the Pirandello ideal of a transfer of action.[23] The characters are drawn principally from the townspeople and peasants
of the Andalusian countryside and provincial circumstances; but
the atmosphere is very contemporary with references to problems, such as the commune experiments of Fourier, the republican political successes and failures, and a fervid defense of Spain,
materially backward and morally superior. One story yields to
another—one enters in another—as the plot shifts back and forth
with some Gothic elements, such as a repulsive beggar, and a
murder, which becomes the focal point of the following se-
quences. Again, Fernán Caballero, experimenting with the
epistolary novel, has moved into the area of the murder mystery.
This time, unlike *The Star of Vandalia,* the action is rendered
very plausible and the story is narrated with verisimilitude,
although the device of coincidence is ultimately the explanatory
trait of the argument. Manuel Díaz, finding a passport on a
corpse, enters a town with his new name of José Ramos and
leads a respectable, prosperous life. He has, however, murdered
out of vengeance the father of Diego Mena who, as a boy,
witnessed his parent's death. Diego is planning to marry Pastora,
the daughter of Díaz, now Ramos; but at the moment of receiving
the latter's blessing for the nuptials, Diego exposes the murderer. The results are tragic for all concerned: Díaz is executed,
Diego and Pastora eventually go insane from the shock of the
truth. There is, in fact, a double murder within the entire novel;
and the suspense and uncertainty about the solutions, added to
the interlocking connections of the episodes (one in another),
form a contrapuntal plot. Thus, from the viewpoint of experi-
mentation and technical virtuosity, Fernán Caballero, happily
leaving aside *costumbrista* sketches and obvious moralizing
phrases in this novelistic work, has perhaps reached a peak of
Realistic enterprise. She has certainly demonstrated a prevailing concern for structure and an approach to narration beyond
the linear or strictly chronological.[24]

Unfortunately, Fernán Caballero's interest in different avenues
to the widening highways of the Realistic novel, and Realism in
general, cannot compete—as has been observed in her previous
works—with the ideological, perhaps psychological, spirit of her

art. Thus, in *Lady Virginia,* the story and themes are dog-
matically oriented toward an attack on foreigners, especially the
British way of life, and the Protestant religion as unsatisfactory
in comparison with Catholicism. Lady Virginia has an illegitimate child (with the less than subtle repetition that an English-
woman, not a Spanish lady, would be guilty of such a breach
of morality!); and after this child's and the father's deaths, she
goes to a small town in Andalucía where the influence of the
virtuous life of the peasants leads her to become a Catholic.

Con mal o con bien a los tuyos te ten (*Stay with your Own in
Good and Bad*) is the tragedy of Regla who, after her father,
a picador, has died in the bullring, marries the dashing Servando
Ramos instead of her faithful cousin, Sebastián. Regla's life is
unhappy: her husband dies in debtors' prison in England where
the two of them have gone to live; and she is compelled to
reject help from Monsieur Folichon, supposedly a friend, because he really wants to seduce her. Returning with her two
children to the charitable shores of Spain after the sad residence
among the inhospitable English, Regla dies in the presence of
Sebastián. Although a cripple, Sebastián promises to care for
her son, the daughter being raised by another generous Spanish
person. Fernán Caballero's religious preoccupation about *una
buena muerte* ("a good death"), as in the climactic scene in *The
Sea Gull* with Pedro Santaló's death, begins to appear frequently,
then, in these short novels.

In *Las dos gracias o la expiación* (*The Two Graces or Expiation*), the theme, providing a dramatic ending to the story and also
a vivid lesson in adherence to orthodoxy, is expressed with an
unusual, for Fernán Caballero, touch of the macabre. Gracia
Vargas is the "good Gracia" and Gracia López is the "bad
Gracia"; and the lives of these "two Gracias," with Gracia López
outwitting her more honest, noble namesake by trickery and
deceit, finally end with the slow, painful death from cancer of
the "bad Gracia." Alfonso, cheated from marriage to Gracia
Vargas by the other girl's tampering with the words of a letter,
refuses at first to forgive Gracia López on the latter's deathbed.
But he is shocked into Christian forgiveness by this gruesome
sight in the hospital room:

Alfonso approached the night table, lifted the towel, and drew
back with an exclamation of astonishment and horror. On the night

table was an arm with the hand inert, cold, and dead. The arm had been severed from the body during the past night because of the progress of the cancer, which had destroyed all the nerves and ligaments of this right arm; and now, like a skeleton, the arm rested there. (III, 389)

The dying moments of Gracia López and the religious ceremonies after her death are described from two orientations: the punishment for her sins and the merits accumulated by those who have forgiven her, and the advocacy of Christian—more specifically, Catholic—rites as the best preparation for "a good death." Fernán Caballero, at any rate, endeavors to link her ideological and literary purposes as she explains in the novel's last sentence: "It is for certain that the dénouement of our love affairs has been neither fictional nor sentimental, and the novel whose function is to create would reject it as prosaic; but the sketch or novel of customs would admit it at once, whose object it is to paint things as they really are" (II, 392).

In *Vulgaridad y nobleza* (*Vulgarity and Nobility*), Fernán Caballero expresses her thesis that "the antithesis of vulgarity is nobility, of which a French author has said that, after sanctity, it is the most beautiful flowering of the soul. But how lost it is! Let us go to seek it. Shall we be able to find it? We shall not find it, certainly, so close at hand as we have found vulgarity" (III, 402).

And, of course, the nineteenth century is fostering vulgarity, according to Fernán Caballero, in a common refrain by now about the decline in moral standards. Also, throughout these novels, briefly and almost like asides, the United States is emerging as the center of the materialism and obsession about money, characteristic of her century, as the author insists sadly. However, she does make a favorable mention occasionally of American literature, and Longfellow is quoted twice, for example, in *The Star of Vandalia*.[25] The plot of *Vulgarity and Nobility* has been somewhat employed previously: the murder of two innocent peasants is revealed accidentally after many years when their graves are found, and the resulting shock exposes the frayed consciences of the guilty parties. In short, justice always triumphs, and the hand of God (the uncovered hand of one of the corpses leads to the discovery of the burial sites) points to sinners even though time may have appeared to save them from exposure. The structure of this *novela corta* is likewise very familiar: a leisurely development of the action, leading suddenly to a dramatic conclusion, which also employs coincidence to solve the problem.

The last short novel, happily, is one of Fernán Caballero's most successful books, popularly and critically. *La farisea* (*The Woman of the Pharisees*) is a character study—or a study in physiology—of Bibiana, a woman related to Marisalada and Rita in Fernán Caballero's two major books. Bibiana is only interested in herself, in her own social progress, and is psychologically unable to interest herself in anything or anyone else, as the author incisively describes her antiheroine immediately in *The Woman of the Pharisees*. Almost for the only time in her works, Fernán Caballero, in her last published novel, makes use of her Puerto Rican experiences as material for the setting of this story. Don Agustín Campos, an officer stationed in Puerto Rico, marries rather surprisingly Bibiana Fajardo because everyone considered them as having very different personalities and attitudes. Luciano Encina, in particular, disapproved quietly and subtly the marriage of his commander; but the young officer, loyal to his chief, follows him throughout the vicissitudes of military service in the morass of nineteenth-century Spanish politics. Bibiana, of course, only married the older man to escape a boring present situation with little expectations for the future. Throughout the succeeding years, Campos climbs the ladder of promotions; but his wife shows herself more aloof and selfish, and he finally realizes that the marriage was a mistake. The presence and enmity of Luciano are disturbing to Bibiana, and no pretense at politeness can prevent the antipathetical feelings on both sides from erupting into angry words. Disaster strikes Campos when he is exiled to the provinces for his role in one of the complicated military-political imbroglios; and Bibiana, understanding that she would lose all social contacts and prestige by joining her husband in the country, remains in Madrid. Campos dies almost alone and broken spiritually by his wife's neglect; and Luciano, talking with his uncle after the latter's visit to Bibiana's home sometime after his superior's death, reprimands his relative's praises of the widow by denouncing her, not as "a new type," but as "a very ancient one—a woman of the Pharisees" (III, 346).

In this story, Fernán Caballero has depicted in a very sharp and immediate manner the character of Bibiana; and the effectiveness is enhanced by the absence of intervening passages, expressing the morality of the scenes. Instead, fortunately, the characterization is disclosed through the individual scenes, such as the contrast with Bibiana's sister, Feliciana, in the small town of Hinojosa; the everpresent Luciano, appearing unexpectedly like a voice of conscience; and the gradually revealed deterioration of the marriage of Campos. Actually, the story falls quantitatively within the genre of the short tale, and perhaps thereby Fernán Caballero's success is better explained, because with this economy of words no margin is allowed for verbose digressions and the tedious sermons in heavy prose, by now the acknowledged defect of the aging author.[26]

Her novels, therefore, must be granted that classification, although it is difficult to understand fully that division on the bases of length and subject material. Fernán Caballero has in general repeated a pattern of settings in Andalucía, an extensive introductory chapter describing the physical scene, a leisurely, very often uninteresting pace, an exciting climax, relying on coincidence, and a stern lesson on the meaning of it all for her readers. For example, the Christian (for her, Catholic) importance of "a happy death," the realization that justice triumphs in this life, the value of sacrifice and service, especially for her tragic heroines, and the victory of those who adhere to the past traditions and ideals stand forth very clearly in the novels. The heroines and antiheroines—the latter being far more fascinating—are involved in a series of innovative structures, such as the epistolary format, the autobiographical backgrounds, the interplay of the new age and the decline of the old stability, and the country versus the city. But, in whatever circumstances these feminine characters are located (and they control the action or at the very least remain important actors in the plot), the direction of the novelistic, and especially Realistic, art has been shifted definitely and winningly to this recognized role, though traditional in the heroines and unapprovingly dynamic in the antiheroines, for the woman in the new novel during the second half of the nineteenth century.

CHAPTER 5

Local Color Sketches, Short Stories, and Letters

THE quantity of material, published in a variety of magazines, shows that Fernán Caballero's popularity, during the years after 1850, and especially during the later period, declining physically and artistically, was maintained, perhaps artificially, by a flood of short pieces rather than long works. However, she is still concerned (as previously with the problem of *novelas* and *novelas cortas*) with the definition for her writings.[1] For example, she now endeavors to classify some stories as *relaciones*, although she is not sure about any precise traits for these "relations." Of course, as Fernán Caballero explains in an introductory note on this issue, any writing must have an ethical part—the former emphasis again on the didactic and moralizing—and the stories must be truthful, if not in all details, certainly at least on the basis of the main outlines of the plot, background, and characters. Now, however, she seemingly wants to broaden her techniques:

The compositions that the French and Germans call *Nouvelles*, and that we, through lack of another more adequate word, call *Relaciones*, differ from the novels of customs (*romans de moeurs*, which are essentially an analysis of the heart and psychological studies) in that they are composed of facts rapidly threaded into the fabric of a narration; this is to say, in that they are water colors instead of miniatures as the aforementioned.

The *Relaciones* (*Relations*) can, in favor of their tendency to *cause an effect*, be emancipated with more ease than the novels of customs from strict probability without adulterating their essence or failing in their object. (II, 303)

I The Relaciones

Within this generalized, and perhaps uncertain, probing into an adequate classification emerges an effort to achieve a surprise ending, a characteristic of the short story in many instances during the nineteenth century, and the aim of causing an effect appears close to Poe's idea.[2] Grouped with this rudimentary category of *relaciones* are nine stories, which resemble nevertheless previous works of Fernán Caballero. *Callar en vida y perdonar en muerte* (*Silence in Life and Pardon in Death*) traces the history of a crime, apparently concealed successfully from the authorities, by a husband who learns on his wife's deathbed that she has known intuitively that he is the real criminal. Her silence, the result also of lack of any positive evidence about the murder, is due overwhelmingly to her loyalty to her spouse and a religious faith: "*'Silence in life,* because I was a mother, and *pardon in death,* because I am a Christian!'* replied the holy martyr, closing her eyes to open them again no more" (II, 249). This short story—because the *relación* so closely fits within the length of the genre—possesses a dramatic and interesting quality, marred in great measure by the moralizing, religious solution imposed so suddenly in the concluding lines. *No transige la conciencia* (*No Compromise with Conscience*) is once again the expression of a favorite theme of Fernán Caballero: "A secret guilt, causing terrible consequences, connected to one another like a group of serpents, had already cost happiness and life to the one who committed it" (II, 268) ... "the horrible secret that oppressed him and involved all his children with him as the terrible serpent makes a prisoner of the father and his children in the magnificent group of Laocoön" (II, 269). However, the ending is happier (with another familiar literary device in the serenity of a Christian or "happy" death) because a father finds in his last moments that his three sons love him equally and that, therefore, he does not have to reveal which one of them is illegitimate—"a sorrowful secret" he has borne for so many years.

La flor de las ruinas (*The Flower of Ruins*), a tragic account of love, narrates the fate of a young girl whom Pedro is determined to marry despite his lack of knowledge about her past and family. The girl's brothers are outlaws who follow the pair and who intend to kill Pedro; but the girl (she is given no name except "the flower of ruins" in the narration) alerts the authorities about the planned murder. She, however, is killed by her brothers; they are executed; and Pedro is fatally afflicted by a brain fever. *Los dos amigos* (*The Two Friends*), based seemingly on the true fate of the Spanish poet, José Cadalso, shows how two friends, Félix and Ramiro, both officers during a siege of Gibraltar in 1782, exchange duty assignments with each other; and one of the friends is killed in an unexpected enemy attack. Ramiro had made a date with a girl friend, but he received orders to command an outpost on that same evening; and Félix immediately offered to take his friend's place. Ramiro's happiness is shattered on the following morning when news of Félix' death is brought to him; and many years afterwards, in 1833, an old Capuchin monk is revealed to be Ramiro, who devotes his life to a humble, prayerful existence, as a Spaniard explains to an Englishman:

"Seeing," finally added the Spaniard, "with so much clarity the finger of God, who was punishing him with such a frightful catastrophe, beside himself with sorrow for having caused by his criminal passion his friend's death, Don Ramiro de Lérida only saw two alternatives: to die or to do penance. Thank God he was a Christian and had sufficient courage to choose the latter." (II, 291)

La hija del sol (*The Daughter of the Sun*), according to a note of Fernán Caballero, is a true *relación,* and she mentions the nun's name and dates, referring also to the common knowledge in Andalusian gossip about the story. The theme, introduced by a quotation from the author's favorite, Balzac ("Is it true? Yes, but what does it matter?"), deals with the illicit love of "the daughter of the sun," so called for her striking beauty, for a young officer. The action, taking place in Sevilla, develops quickly and dramatically: the absence of the heroine's (or antiheroine's) husband, whom she married out of duty rather than for love, results in a love affair with Don Carlos de las Navas. One night, however, two assassins kill the young man; and "the daughter of the sun," helped by her servant, takes the corpse to a distant place to avoid scandal. But on the following day, the military parade, at which her lover usually took part, again comes past the guilty wife's house; and she sees in horror her paramour. The shock of this inexplicable event (impossible to unfathom for unbelievers, according to Fernán Caballero) makes the famous beauty fall ill, confess later her guilt to her husband, and retire for the remainder of her life to a convent. This Sevillian legend—somewhat like the *leyendas* of Bécquer[3]—is the most mysterious of Fernán Caballero's many stories and is also the one most solidly rooted in fact (if the source is accurate).

The two *relaciones, Justa y Rufina* and *Más largo es el tiempo que la fortuna (Time Is Longer than Fortune)*, as Fernán Caballero indicates, form a contrasting pair of stories: the former illustrates the vice of envy destroying the happiness of Justa because of Rufina's actions; and the latter again traces the idea of the justice of God triumphing over the wiles of men who have broken the moral law. In the first story, Rufina is so entrapped from childhood by her envious nature that she causes misfortune for everyone, including her child and her innocent rival, Justa. Rufina, jealous of Justa's baby, exchanges her own daughter for the latter's; and in later life, when an unexpected inheritance comes to Justa's real child, Rufina cannot psychologically confess the truth. Justa dies poor, Rufina lives a life of wealth; but eventually the latter squanders all her resources, and she dies, repeating the word, "mercy." In the second *relación*, time is synonymous with justice, and fortune designates the long enjoyment of ill-gained wealth, power, and prestige—with the eventual revelation of the truth, through coincidence and conscience as the literary and ideological techniques, respectively. Juan Luis Navajas betrays his ally, José Camas, by murdering the latter's father and running away with the old man's money; he also manages to have the guilt point to José, the murdered man's son. The true criminal, under the assumed name of Víctor Guerra, goes to the army where he wins promotions easily. However, old Bernardo, the friend of the murdered innkeeper, pursues the guilty Navajas; and the latter, so disturbed by the discovery of the past, flees to the United States where he dies in a brawl, an appropriate punishment for his life of crime. The second *relación*, similar in theme and structure with some of the previous *novelas cortas*, adds little to the artistic progression of Fernán Caballero; but the story of *Justa y Rufina*, although a lengthier treatment might have contributed an impressive psychological novel (if the author could have resisted too many moralizing digressions), probes deftly and in various facets the problem of envy, such as Unamuno attempted in his "nivola," *Abel Sánchez*.

Estar de más (To Be in the Way), however, fails to sustain the innovative glimpses into Realism because the argument is simply the theme of Enoch Arden: a wife, believing her first husband to have died at sea, remarries; and the missing spouse, returning after many years, knows that he has "to be in the way," if he remains. Quite characteristically for Fernán Caballero, the solution for the first husband is to retire gracefully to a religious house where he dies after leading a solitary, exemplary life.

Magdalena presents another unfavorable picture of a foreigner, an English noble (perhaps a literary revenge on "Federico Cuthbert"), who seduces, with the help of a nineteenth-century Celestina, Magdalena, the sister of Fernando, who kills "lord G." and stoically accepts his own execution for redeeming the family honor—another theme seen previously in Fernán Caballero's works, and certainly an idea important in the *comedia* of the Golden Age.

II *Local Color Sketches*

If the distinctions between the *relaciones, novelas,* and *novelas cortas* are not precisely determined, the dividing line with the local color sketches is likewise unmapped territory. For example, there are *costumbrista* qualities in the nine *relaciones*: the Andalusian settings, the folklore bases for many of the narrations, the wisdom of the peasants, the prevailing belief in the eventual victory of divine justice, and the everpresent religious orientations of the characters as well as the themes.

Still, Fernán Caballero strives to separate the local color sketches from the genre of stories; and one should at least take into account her attempt to move in the direction of a theory of Realism, or the new writing of the later nineteenth century:

Some think—led to it without doubt by the denomination of popular which our local color sketches bear—that we reproduce them for the people, and this is an error that is demonstrated with only the simple objection that the people whom we paint do not read. . . . We shall add only one word. It has been also thought that we invent the stories, sayings, songs, and comparisons which we made into our popular sketches. It is so beyond us to give as our own what is not, that many times we have repeated that the merit which these sketches can and do have really is none other than the true and genuine, which they are at heart, in the details, descriptions, ideas, and language.

It is sufficient to stop for an instant in order to know the source

from which they spring. Culture does not have primitive innocence
and candor; it lacks independent and original witticism; its polished
language does not have energy and concision—and thus it lacks also
liberty in expression—of the old and robust religious sentiments that
the people still maintain; all of which, for better or for worse, these
sketches reproduce. (IV, 77)

These local color sketches, then, have as a guiding principle
a less dramatic movement because of their quality as an exact
and true reproduction of the life, traditions, and history of the
common people of Andalucía. There is, instead of emphasis on
form and style, a pervading sentiment of the religious and
national heritage. The question arises, however, about the artistry
of such a literary thesis in achieving contemporary interest and
permanent merits for pieces of literature.[4]

Fernán Caballero's innovations, or endeavors to develop a
distinctly original prose direction, consisting in the first place
as a break with Romanticism, extend to what she defines (likewise vaguely without any manifesto as in the important prologue
to *The Sea Gull*) as simply *Diálogos* (*Dialogues*). Six stories,
unrelated and independent in plot and characters, are grouped
nevertheless under the proverbial generalization of *Cosa cumplida
...sólo en la otra vida* (*A Thing Fulfilled...Only in the Other
Life*). The structure of these "dialogues" resembles the model of
Don Juan Manuel's *Conde Lucanor* (*Count Lucanor*) in the
fourteenth century, where the nobleman and his adviser, Patronio,
provide a frame of reference, introducing the story, and finally,
summing up the moral at the end. Fernán Caballero's Marquesa
de Alora, "young, pretty, and happy," together with her old
friend, the Count of Viana, talk initially about the vagaries and
mysteries of life, an example of the particular issue is mentioned,
and then the meaning or application is inserted as a finale.
However, all the six stories illustrate the thesis of the general
title: God's ways are always just, although the understanding of
the twisted destinies of men is not revealed often until much
later, or even after death. Faith and stoicism, together with
humility and honor, are demanded by daily circumstances of the
stalwart Andalusian peasants, whom Fernán Caballero depicts
in these sketches. *El albañil* (*The Mason*), *El marinero* (*The
Sailor*), *El sochantre de lugar* (*The Village Subchanter*), *El
general* (*The General*), *El quinto* (*The Draftee*), and *Un tío en*

América (*An Uncle in America*) vary in quality and effectiveness; and *El sochantre de lugar* has been recognized as the most outstanding of the six "dialogues"—it is also the longest of the narrations—because of the technical aspects as a *cuadro de costumbres,* according to the author.[5]

A clue, perhaps, to Fernán Caballero's studies of character, or physiologies of Balzac, may be gleamed from the individual titles in the *diálogos.* Each person, especially the village choir singer, is buffeted by either adverse events, or quite simply, the usual tragedies of human existence, such as death of a loved one. The religious influence emerges when each person reacts as Job; and this thematic influence coincides with Fernán Caballero's defense of the traditional spirit of the rural inhabitants of Andalusian towns and countryside. However, the mood of these six vignettes seems to revert to the form of the essay or the local color sketches during the heyday of *costumbrismo* before 1850. The absence of conflict, plot complications, but the perennial (repeated in the same form in the six "dialogues") moral about the labyrinthine paths of divine intervention result in a literary endeavor, interesting principally as an innovative work within the author's total production.[6]

Two other examples of this literary genre (accepting Fernán Caballero's explanations) in which a characterization represents a combination of the Job-like attitude and the stoical posture of the Andalusian type are *Simón Verde* and *Lucas García.* Simón Verde, after suffering financial losses and harassment because of his kindness and Christian charity, forgives his enemy, the mayor, on the latter's deathbed; and the hero lives out the rest of his few remaining years, vindicated and happy because of his daughter's successful marriage. Lucas García, like Simón Verde, prefers to suffer in silence rather than to surrender his honor—or his stubborn interpretation of his honor. Thus, Lucas García, objecting to his father's remarriage to a young girl, leaves the town and joins the army; he even refuses his recognition to his sister, Lucía, when she appears at the military post with her suitor, the commanding officer. Only at the end, after many bitter years, does Lucas return to the village and is reconciled with his sister—through his acceptance of the Christian message of love, forgiveness, and charity. In both stories, the plot solutions are resolved in a laudatory, moralizing manner by the triumph of

Christian ideals over the traits, noble at times but subject to the wrong interpretations of human nature, of the townspeople and peasantry in Andalucía.

El último consuelo (*The Last Consolation*) portrays the grief of a mother about her criminal son, who has as a fugitive lost his life in a quicksand trap; but the mother's sorrow is turned into religious consolation by the report that her son died with his hands formed as a cross, indicating thereby his repentance. *Dicha y suerte* (*Happiness and Luck*) contrasts the two themes: Vicente, returning blind from the war, wins Rosa despite his poverty and physical handicap, while Don Próspero is unhappy despite his wealth. *Más vale honor que honores* (*Honor Is Worth More Than Honors*) is one of the weakest stories of Fernán Caballero because she drifts into the sentimental literature of the *feuilleton* with a plot complicated by unmotivated and coincidental revelations of the true parentage of the characters, and with very overt references to the liberal politicians and military interventions.[7] *Obrar bien . . . que Dios es Dios* (*To Act Well . . . For God Is God*) returns to Dos Hermanas as the setting and, within a very short piece, inserts a popular children's tale; but the plot, dealing with a priest's successful protection of a young girl against a soldier's designs, is no more than a façade for the obvious moral. *El dolor es una agonía sin muerte* (*Sorrow Is an Agony Without Death*) describes a mother's fatal shock upon seeing her missing son return unexpectedly.

III   Relatos Breves

The series of *relatos breves* (*Short Stories*) again do not fall readily and conveniently into any set classification; and Fernán Caballero's subtitle for one story as a *proverbio en acción* ("proverb in action") refers perhaps to an element or motive common to all the narrations. Two seemingly independent local color sketches, *La noche de Navidad* (*Christmas Night*) and *El día de reyes* (*The Feast of the Magi*), connect a semblance of a plot in the absence and disunity of a family, brought together after six years by dint of the religious holidays. *El ex-voto* (*The Ex-Vow*) shows the power of religious symbolism when a murderer, driven to crime by the desire to obtain money for marriage to a village girl, is hindered by the entanglement of a cross with his weapon. The story is marred by a slow opening, with adverse comments on the English as individuals and their occupation of Gibraltar, in addition to several references to folklore without a clear link to the action; and the finale is more in accord with a *relación*, since an effect is the concluding result.[8] *Matrimonio bien avenido, la mujer junto al marido* (*In a Harmonious Marriage, the Wife Is at the Side of her Husband*) presents a single excursion of Fernán Caballero into the dramatic formula; and her *entremés*, or short dramatic piece, is farcical as two wives pursue their absent husbands to the city of Cádiz.

However, the vein of observation and narration mined so assiduously and winningly in her early days now remained secondary to her concentration upon the purely descriptive, in essays of her travels, and upon the legendary, always with stress on the moralizing and religious values of the particular effort. Thus, *Promesa de un soldado a la Virgen del Carmen* (*Promise of a Soldier to the Virgin of Mount Carmel*) is a devout legend of a soldier's salvation by his wearing of a religious medal. Briefly, as in *Deudas pagadas* (*Paid Debts*), where Fernán Caballero tries to reconcile traditional virtues, such as honor, patriotism, and loyalty, with her opposition to the conscription of peasants, she shows how the Spanish wars in Africa, though favored by some nationalistic elements, do not bring true glory and honest prestige to the nation. In "Paid Debts," the mother's tears and complaints, while they win concessions from the favorably portrayed officers for her son, are more indicative of a poor, simple countrywoman's anguish. It is in these two brief glimpses at a contemporary issue, and crisis, of the nineteenth century that Fernán Caballero, as in her longer works, demonstrates that she was aware of and able to depict these problems, but that she withdrew from any extensive, highly critical commentaries.

There are the essays, descriptive, impressionistic, and didactic, as *El Alcázar de Sevilla* (*The Alcázar of Seville*) on the history and legends of the ancient fortress; *Un sermón bajo naranjos* (*A Sermon under Orange Trees*) on the religious associations of the Cathedral of Sevilla; *El Eddistone* (*The Eddystone*) on the lighthouse, Eddystone Rock, in the English Channel; *Una excursión a Waterloo* (*An Excursion to Waterloo*) on the horrors of warfare evoked by a visit to the Belgian battlefield; *Aquisgrán* on the historical, cultural beauties of the German city of Aquisgran, Aix-la-Chapelle, or Aachen; *Episodio de un viaje a Carmona* (*Episode of a Trip to Carmona*) on the wise remarks and stoical attitude of peasants coming into fleeting contact with sophisticated foreign travelers; *El vendedor de tagarninas* (*The Oyster Plant Seller*) on a brief glance at the humble, resigned life of this tradesman, with attendant lessons about personal sufferings; *Un naufragio* (*A Shipwreck*) on the heroism of the survivors of a ship during a storm in 1856; *Una visita al convento de Santa Inés de Sevilla* (*A Visit to the Convent of Saint Inés of Seville*) on the contemporary values of the religious life, exemplified by this edifice and the nuns; *La Catedral de Sevilla en una tarde de Carnaval* (*The Cathedral of Seville on an Afternoon during Carnival*) on the contrasts between the noisy amusements of Carnival and the silence of the church.

In *Una madre* (*A Mother*), Fernán Caballero has successfully blended the historical essay and her familiar elements of the short story, or *relación,* in order to create an effect. The narration is short and dramatic: a mother sees her three sons leave with the ill-fated Spanish fleet for the Battle of Trafalgar, Oct. 20, 1805; and the shock of welcoming, unexpectedly, the three young men, singly, and returning unharmed, results in an ironic tragedy: "That mother's heart, so tender and so suffering, could not stand so much happiness! She had lost her mind!" (IV, 387).

IV *Miscellaneous Writings*

By now, the continued writings of Fernán Caballero, evidently popular, were concentrated principally in magazines and newspapers with emphasis upon the moralizing and religious lessons—and with less artistic merits. The literary yielded increasingly to the ideological, and the reasons for the author's critical decline after 1870, in particular, are evident in the quality of these contributions. However, the quantity of small items is impressive: the proof of long, diligent observations; a retentive memory; and the sincere, fervent love of the folklore, traditions, and history of the Andalusian province.[9]

In the final years, the *relatos breves* appeared sporadically with no variations in technique, however. The moral was, if anything, more obvious; and the defense of ideology more emphatic. For example, *La corruptora y la buena maestra* (*The Corrupting and the Good Teacher*) contrasts the attitudes of two young men, Isidro and Amaro, the former led to goodness by teachers, such as De Maistre, and the latter, led to unhappiness, by models, such as Renan; *La maldición paterna* (*The Paternal Curse*) is a contrived lesson about a son's sudden blindness, his later suffering, and final repentance, after striking his father; *La viuda del cesante* (*The Widow of the Dismissed Public Employee*) presents a vivid, contemporary problem, though tinted by sentimentalism, of the need for a civil service in Spain because of the rapid hirings and firings of governmental personnel after a change of ministries, so frequent in this century, and an issue raised by Galdós in his *novelas contemporáneas* (*Contemporary Novels*); *Las mujeres cristianas* (*The Christian Women*) offers a vignette in defense of the monarchy by showing the generosity of a Princess, Queen Isabel II's sister, to a poor woman and her son; *Leonor* shows the superiority and victory of religious love over human love through the sacrifice and service of the heroine; *Los dos memoriales* (*The Two Memorials*) repeats the theme of the kindness of Queen Isabel II and stresses anew the merits of the monarchy; *Un vestido* (*A Dress*) revolves about a husband's desire for his wife to buy a new dress for his own self-importance and his spouse's use of the money for a mission of Christian charity; *Los pobres perros abandonados* (*The Poor Abandoned Dogs*) is an amusing defense of stray dogs, more appreciated in Spain, according to the author, than in the less hospitable European countries. This last *relato breve* is also an essay in which Cervantes, writing to Fernán Caballero, recognizes her "as the ingenious author of so many novels more exemplary than mine" (V, 57); and the association between this story and the Cervantine exemplary novel, *El coloquio de los perros* (*The Colloquy of the Dogs*) is recalled.

Fernán Caballero collected *Cuentos y poesías populares andaluces* (*Andalusian Popular Poetry and Short Stories*) in which she took pride in an original collection comparing favorably with those of the Grimms, about the wit, humor, and intuitive wisdom of the Andalusian character. She also admits Mazade's analysis as reliable that Spanish Catholicism is an abiding trait and explanation of the folklore and stories.[10] Together with *Cantos, coplas y trobos populares* (*Songs, Popular Songs, and More Popular Songs*) a panorama of the legendary, traditional, and historical roots of the province of Andalucía is unfolded, with a strong quality of the religious faith in overwhelming evidence. Short stories, tales, songs, proverbs, puns, and jokes are offered in these many pages; and the sharp tongue of the peasants, their proud independence, a sense of individuality, and respect for a person who merits such an honor stand out very clearly in the transcriptions. All these qualities, of course, were precisely the attributes sought by Fernán Caballero in her observations, utilized in her earlier works, and defended consistently—and not always impartially—throughout her life. There are likewise in the same vein *Refranes y máximas populares recogidos en los pueblos de campo* (*Refrains and Maxims Collected in the Country Towns*), *Adivinas y acertijos populares* (*Popular Riddles and Puzzles*), *Colección de artículos religiosos y morales* (*Collection of Religious and Moral Articles*), *Pensamientos, máximas, definiciones por varios autores* (*Thoughts, Maxims, Definitions by Various Authors*), and *Refranes* (Refrains). All these items, however, convey the impression of being space fillers for journalistic demands; and Fernán Caballero's difficult financial circumstances, before and after Arrom de Ayala's suicide, probably explain her dedication to this form of writing rather than to her prior, early successes in novels and stories.

Nevertheless, a final, more charming, and happier literary enterprise is Fernán Caballero's contribution to children's reading interests. She makes use of the same observations and wealth of Andalusian folklore, traditions, etc., to create an atmosphere of entertainment, gentle morality, and love of country ways. Her popularity is certainly attested to by the many published pieces, grouped in these collections, *Cuentos, oraciones, adivinas y refranes populares e infantiles* (*Popular and Children's Short Stories, Prayers, Puzzles, and Refrains*) with the *Cuentos de encantamiento* (*Tales of Enchantment*); *Cuentos infantiles religiosos* (*Children's Religious Stories*); *Adivinas infantiles* (*Children's Puzzles*), including the *Solución de las adivinas infantiles* (*Solution of the Children's Puzzles*); *Oraciones, relaciones y coplas infantiles* (*Children's Prayers, Stories, and Songs*); and *Mitología para los niños* (*Mythology for Children*). Although this literature has disappeared from any serious criticism of Fernán Caballero's works, all these productions kept her name in the public view during the declining years, especially after 1870,

when a reaction set in with the appearance of the Realistic novel
in superior examples of Galdós, Valera, etc.

V *The Correspondence*

The shift to letter writing after 1853 and the survival of little
correspondence before that date were previously related in the
first chapter to Fernán Caballero's life as a public figure, whatever her feelings on this attention were, and the need on her
part to defend and to justify her record as author and an advocate
of traditionalism. In fact, the recognition of her correspondence,
stimulated by the publication, generally in fragments and at irreg-
ular intervals, has grown significantly with the attention of critics,
such as Montesinos: "The letters of Fernán Caballero that have
been published are very many. It is a hope that some day, some
friend of this author may make a selection of those papers; well
done, with a gathering together of everything essential, and the
most charming and picturesque, it would be as good as the best
of her novels."[11]

The correspondence, however, is not without critical pitfalls,
the principal trap being this repeated fact that the letters belong
to a period considerably after the inception, first drafts, and
formalized orientations of the author, and when her best work
had been published. But the explanations of technical problems,
such as editing, the uncertainties of acceptance by publishers, the
fears about the possible delays in the appearance of the works,
the reactions to critics, and, of course, the invaluable attempts to
understand, to define, and to win support of the new novel and
the incompletely understood Realism provide one of the most
significant contributions to epistolary literature of the nineteenth
century. A determination to express herself, a belief in the merits
of her writings, and a recognition of her role as an important
figure in Spanish literature of the nineteenth century become
inescapable conclusions of this correspondence.

At the same time, the proclaimed modesty and request for
anonymity appear paradoxical in view of the continued publications, letters, and contents of this correspondence. This attitude is
really eclectic: she insisted upon the maintenance of the traditional feminine traits—a theme in many of the letters—with the
choice and the right for herself to play a role, personally and
artistically, in Spanish life. She is really pursuing a middle path

between the ostentatious "emancipated woman" or "free woman," as the denigrating term is repeated often in her writings, a product of the nineteenth century, distasteful and insulting, and the Spanish woman, who exemplifies the prime qualities of a wife and mother. But, in order to expound her thesis, Fernán Caballero went against the grain of her literary ideal: she is, in her compromising, forward-and-retreat manner, with "two steps forward and one step backward," advancing diplomatically in the direction of feminism, which term, nevertheless, she would have opposed. An overt, blatant appearance, especially in Spain, would have aroused furious opposition not only from a male-dominated literary establishment but also from her own sympathizers, the conservative, feminine audience. Here is perhaps an explanation, in some measure, for her insistence upon the correct reaction to her ideas, the anger at critics and reviewers who tried to insert more advanced theories, in accord with nineteenth-century European experiments, and the continued philosophy of traditionalism, religious, social, and political.

Nevertheless, the correspondence is the best biography of Fernán Caballero in terms of her personal struggles, conflicting emotions, and anguished insecurity as a writer and a woman. She shows herself a sensitive, sincere person who can fight repeatedly and arduously for her independence. Also, she is no impartial critic, complaining bitterly and stridently on many an occasion about a supposed injustice. Her stalwart ideological posture carries over to her demand for recognition; and she is harsh about any negative remarks about her life, particularly in the later attacks upon her intrusion—denied by her—into the political confrontations between liberals and conservatives. Indeed, this lack of moderation and balance about differing opinions emerges as a factor in her plummeting reputation about 1870, and more sharply after her death. All in all, however, the positive values of the correspondence, about the theories of the new novel and the direction of nineteenth-century Spanish literature, compensate for the dogmatic, overly sensitive, and biased judgments of the many letters, a sign, on the other hand, of a many-sided personality.

CHAPTER 6

Influence and Critical Fortune

THE general theory of Fernán Caballero about the Realistic novel, or the new novel of the second half of the nineteenth century, as she better understood or certainly defined the issue, has been summarized and popularized in literary histories by the phrase, *La novela no se inventa, se observa* ("The novel is not invented, it is observed"). Her pioneership and leadership, the latter subdued and unfortunately never exploited adequately, were recognized immediately and without opposition, mainly under the influence of Ochoa's praise of the "Spanish Sir Walter Scott," after the publication of *The Sea Gull* in 1849. The continued plaudits ironically came from the literary establishment, which Fernán Caballero feared and courted simultaneously; and her succeeding works, stimulated by Hartzenbusch's faithful help, were characteristically introduced with prologues by recognized figures, such as the Duque de Rivas, for the book publication of *The Family of Alvareda*. There are consequently successive names of critics, important and influential in this period, 1850-1870, who lent their weight to Fernán Caballero's fame. A glance, however, at these sources and their remarks shows a consistent pattern of adherence to the author's traditionalism, morality, and ideology; and, in short, no adverse, or even impartial, critiques emerge from the introductory pages. Good luck also marked Fernán Caballero's popularity during these twenty years because no serious, worthwhile opposition existed from other novelists, and she is therefore the only Spanish novelist still known as meritorious during the two decades after the first half of the ninetenth century.[1]

By 1870, however, the aging and virtually retired author, who had erred by not leading more forcefully (with subtle public gestures to allay her own conservative constituency) the Realistic Movement she so obviously represented, faced two challenges: the collapse of the political ideas she espoused,

156

symbolized in the monarchy, especially of Isabel II, by the whirl-wind of the years, 1868-1876; and the appearance of Realism in vigor, particularly with Galdós. Fernán Caballero almost dis-appeared at first from any respectful recall as a great novelist—or the creator of the modern Spanish novel—and, generally perhaps because of her death in 1877, when Spain returned to the governmental stability she favored, under Alfonso XII, she was remembered in a national homage (convenient for the young, shaky régime). Of more certain explanation, nevertheless, is the clear fact of the Spanish novel, prospering and expanding in popular and critical terms. The Spanish novel, however, was now diverging into two main currents: the regional novel, the ideal of Fernán Caballero; and the more European, more liberal, productions of Galdós (and Valera, to some extent). The region-alists—and this term is imprecise—favored the country, traditions, conservatism in government and society, and clericalism. These novelists defended and praised Fernán Caballero; and the names are of course noteworthy: Pedro Antonio de Alarcón, José María de Pereda, and Emilia Pardo Bazán, the latter a fellow woman novelist and the eclectic initiator of Naturalism.[2] But the oppo-sition is undoubtedly more formidable and impressive: Galdós, who accepted Fernán Caballero's role as a pioneer but balked strongly at her sermonizing; Valera, who attacked urbanely her falsified, idealized Andalusian settings; and Marcelino Menén-dez Pelayo, caught between his fame as the prestigious critic and yet the sympathizer with the author's ideological view-points, finally effected in 1884 (for a prologue to the complete works of Pereda, surely no accident) an analysis based on her considerable merits as the initiator of the modern Spanish novel of customs and ruralism, granting at the same time the objec-tions about the limited scope of her plots and characters, in addition to the well-intentioned sermons. Indeed, Menéndez Pelayo's criticism has survived very successfully for a near century in the many literary histories; and his arguments are really open to no serious challenge, presenting as they do opin-ions, balanced, studied, and objective.[3]

Still, Fernán Caballero's reputation suffered a further decline in the general onslaught of the Generation of 1898 against the preceding literature of the nineteenth century; and the most devastating attacks seem to be those of Pío Baroja—appropriately enough, the acclaimed iconoclast of this entire group of young rebels against the disasters in all aspects of their nation. Naturalism, in the more authoritative tones of Clarín, attacked Fernán Caballero for her portrayals—and omissions—about the life of the countryside and the peasants; and the Generation of 1898 found an influential source of the Spanish miasma in the ideology of Fernán Caballero, accepted by the discredited governments of the Bourbon monarchy. These barbs dominated Spanish criticism of Fernán Caballero until the end of World War I when, ironically, respect for her contributions came from abroad. Benedetto Croce and George Santayana wrote favorably, as critic and reader, respectively; and it is significant to remember that Fernán Caballero attained early fame and respect outside Spain during her lifetime, which of course may have helped her reputation in the country. Her popular and critical support in Germany, France, England, and the United States, in that descending order, respectively, for her works in the original Spanish, translations, or school texts is additional, welcome, and yet surprising acknowledgment for Fernán Caballero as an established, major writer of Spain.[4]

Undoubtedly, the continuing publication of Fernán Caballero's correspondence has supplied a secure, scholarly basis for more learned studies and, in turn, a more sympathetic attitude toward her additions to the modern Spanish novel. A surge of interest and investigations about Romanticism in Spain, shortly before World War II, likewise led to the inclusion and recognition of Fernán Caballero, perhaps at first indirectly because of Böhl von Faber's participation in the movement, as an offshoot of the early nineteenth-century literary school and ideas. A general thesis about Fernán Caballero, proceeding in some degree from Menéndez Pelayo's earlier conclusions, appears to be that she deserves more respect within the framework of literary history rather than as a master of the Spanish novel during the nineteenth century, or as the author of a single, outstanding masterpiece outside the total reference of Spanish literature.

Therefore, Cecilia Böhl de Faber, more popularly known by her pseudonym of Fernán Caballero, is the creator of the modern Spanish novel and the first important novelist who successfully directed this genre from Romanticism toward Realism after 1850. She also emerges in this study as the first feminist of modern Spanish literature and as an equal of her contemporaries, George Sand and George Eliot. Her literary friendship with Washington Irving during the latter's residence in Spain (1828-1829) provided encouragement and stimulus for some important early writings. This period before the publication of *The Sea Gull* (1849) and *The Family of Alvareda* (1856), her two major novels, shows that Fernán Caballero had prepared many compositions long before their appearance in magazines and books. Her father, a famous German Hispanist living in Spain, and her Spanish mother, a bold advocate of women's rights, also encouraged the young writer. Fernán Caballero's personal life, tragic and somewhat obscure primarily because of the deaths of three husbands, is nonetheless revealing about this unusual woman's inner strength and artistic persistence. She dominated popularly and critically the Spanish novel during the otherwise barren period from 1850 until 1870 when Realism will begin to triumph, thanks in large part to the literary career of this woman with the masculine pen name, Fernán Caballero.

Notes and References

Chapter One

1. The most reliable and extensive sources of biographical information are: Fernando de Gabriel y Ruiz de Apodaca, *Estar de más, relación, y Magdalena, obra inédita, precedidas de una noticia biográfica* (Sevilla: Gironés y Orduña, 1878); and José María Asensio, "Fernán Caballero y la novela contemporánea," *Obras completas* (Madrid: Colección de Escritores Castellanos, 1893), the prologue to Volume I.

2. Javier Herrero, *Fernán Caballero: un nuevo planteamiento* (Madrid: Editorial Gredos, 1963), has devoted the first of the three parts of his study to an investigation of the Böhl von Faber marriage, and the enforced separations of husband and wife with their respective careers.

3. *Ibid.*, pp. 60-71.

4. Camille Pitollet, *La Querelle Caldéronienne de Johan Nikolas Böhl von Faber et José Joaquín de Mora* (Paris: Félix Alcan, 1909), stresses the German Hispanist's enthusiasm as a literary and religious convert to the Hispanic world.

5. The source for Böhl von Faber's remarks about his marriage is traced to two rare volumes: Elisa Campe, *Versuch einer Lebensskizze von Johan Nikolas Böhl von Faber nach seinen eigenen Briefen* (Leipzig, 1858); Johannes Dornhof, *Johann Nikolaus Böhl von Faber: Ein Vorkämpfer der Romantik in Spanien* (Hamburg, 1922). Herrero and Pitollet have indicated the main features of these two books in their biographical summaries.

6. This thesis has been pointed out by Herrero as an essential argument about Fernán Caballero's background.

7. Alfred Morel-Fatio, "Fernán Caballero d'après so correspondance avec Antoine de Latour," *Bulletin Hispanique*, III (1901), 152-294, also refers to this explanation in his survey of the letters.

8. Herrero in his thorough analysis, and José María Castro Calvo in his "estudio preliminar," *Obras de Fernán Caballero* (Madrid: Biblioteca de Autores Españoles, 1961), I, lean to the view that the marital tensions were quite serious.

9. Herrero, pp. 38-39.

10. *Ibid.*, pp. 118-41.

11. British Hispanism has provided authoritative investigations on the roots, growth, and chronology of Spanish Romanticism: Ivy L. McClelland, *The Origins of the Romantic Movement in Spain* (Liverpool: Institute of Hispanic Studies, 1937); E. Allison Peers, *A History of the Romantic Movement in Spain* (Cambridge: Cambridge University Press, 1940), 2 vols.; and F. Courtney Tarr, *Romanticism in Spain and Spanish Romanticism* (Liverpool: Institute of Hispanic Studies, 1939).

12. Pitollet's book on the "Calderonian Quarrel" is the definitive work on this decisive confrontation between the Neoclassical and Romantic points of view.

13. Morel-Fatio, pp. 270-71.

14. Chapters eight and nine of *Clemencia*, Part I, should be read in conjunction with the facts of Fernán Caballero's first marriage, pp. 36-45, in the B. A. E. *Obras*, II.

15. Herrero, pp. 153-54.

16. José F. Montesinos, *Fernán Caballero. Ensayo de justificación* (México: El Colegio de México, 1961), pp. 141-78, has traced thoroughly the "cronología y bibliografía" of Fernán Caballero's works.

17. *Ibid.*, p. 5.

18. Camille Pitollet, "Les premiers essais littéraires de Fernán Caballero," *Bulletin Hispanique*, IX (1907), 67-86, 286-302; X (1908), 286-305, 378-96.

19. Claude G. Bowers, *The Spanish Adventures of Washington Irving* (Boston: Houghton Mifflin, 1940); Stanley T. Williams, *The Life of Washington Irving* (New York: Oxford University Press, 1935) and *The Spanish Background of American Literature* (New Haven: Yale University Press, 1955), II, 3-45, present the overall picture of Irving's two residences in Spain, particularly the first and more impressionable visit.

20. Clara L. Penney, *Washington Irving Diary, Spain 1828-1829* (New York: The Hispanic Society of America, 1930), pp. 89-90.

21. Stanley T. Williams, "Washington Irving and Fernán Caballero," *Journal of English and Germanic Philology*, XXIX (1930), 359-60.

22. *Ibid.*, p. 360.

23. Herrero, *Fernán Caballero*, pp. 200-217, considers that this episode is central to the composition of *Clemencia*, "one of the best novels of the XIXth century" (p. 216), basing his conclusions on the findings of Santiago Montoto, *Cartas inéditas de Fernán Caballero* (Madrid: S. Aguirre Torre, 1961), first published in the *Boletín de la Real Academia Española* from 1955 to 1960.

24. *Ibid.*, p. 530.

25. Theodor Heinermann, *Cecilia Böhl de Faber (Fernán Caba-*

llero) *y Juan Eugenio Hartzenbusch. Una correspondencia inédita* (Madrid: Espasa-Calpe, 1944), pp. 44-46, first develops this argument, although Morel-Fatio, "Les premiers essais littéraires," p. 271, had earlier hinted at this explanation.

26. Montesinos, *Fernán Caballero,* p. 144, reproduces the text.

27. *Ibid.,* p. 96. Montesinos, on several occasions in his book, makes a valid point about the grammatical weaknesses of Fernán Caballero's writings, especially during the early years.

28. Heinermann, Morel-Fatio, and Pitollet show in the published letters that financial problems undoubtedly were a factor in Fernán Caballero's decision.

29. Diego de Valencina, *Cartas de Fernán Caballero* (Madrid: Sucesores de Hernando, 1919), pp. 15-20. The letter, though undated, has been identified convincingly by Valencina as written in 1848.

30. *Obras,* V, 441. The edition of the B. A. E., numbered as volumes CXXXVI, CXXXVII, CXXXVIII, CXXXIX, CXL in the entire collection, is listed for convenience in this book as volumes I-V of the section on Fernán Caballero. All quotations and references to the works, unless indicated otherwise, are placed in parentheses with the volume and page numbers.

31. Luis Coloma, *Recuerdos de Fernán Caballero* (Madrid: Editorial "Razón y Fe," 1949), XVII, 150. Coloma's inventive and mythical remembrances about Fernán Caballero were unfortunately accepted as accurate and reliable for too long by scholarly and popular circles; but his narration is suspect on many grounds, a result of recent publications of the correspondence, in particular. The account is nevertheless somewhat indicative of Fernán Caballero's ideas and may contain some correct motifs.

32. Heinermann, *Cecilia Böhl de Faber (Fernán Caballero),* pp. 59-98, has reproduced the letters of 1849, showing the many anxieties, etc., of the author; and he has also clarified the chronology about *The Sea Gull* in his article, "Dichtung und Wahrheit über die Gaviota Fernán Caballeros," *Romanische Forschungen,* LVI (1942), 313-24.

33. Juan Valera objected to this critique in *The Edinburgh Review,* CXIV (1861), 99-129, pointing out her difficulties in the use of Spanish, and her "Germanic sentimentalism," but admitting her important role in the development of the Spanish novel: Juan Valera, *Obras completas,* XXI (Madrid, 1949), 235.

34. Castro Calvo, "estudio preliminar," p. lii, dedicates a section of his introduction to a summary with abundant quotations from the published correspondence.

35. Heinermann, *Cecilia Böhl de Faber (Fernán Caballero),* p. 97, quoting a letter of July 21, 1849.

36. Herrero and Montesinos, with their biographical and critical

approaches, respectively, coincide, generally speaking, in their independent conclusions about the regrettably late appearance of Fernán Caballero as a Realist upon the European scene.

37. Valencina, *Cartas de Fernán Caballero*, p. 39, quoting a letter of October 15, 1852.

38. Montesinos, *Fernán Caballero*, pp. 141-78; Herrero, *Fernán Caballero*, pp. 269-74.

39. Her annoyance about the choices for foreign audiences appears repeatedly in scattered remarks throughout the various sources of the correspondence during the later years.

40. Fernán Caballero's last, unhappy years were unfortunately a convenient source for sentimental, romantic, and unreliable reports of later biographers, such as Coloma, *Recuerdos de Fernán Caballero*; Angélica Palma, *Fernán Caballero, la novelista novelable* (Madrid: Espasa-Calpe, 1931); Julio Romano, *Fernán Caballero (La alondra y la tormenta)*, Madrid: Editora Nacional, 1949. Fernando de Gabriel y Ruiz de Apodaca and José María Asensio in their biographical material also lost some objectivity in their analyses of Fernán Caballero's final decade of life. A brief but objective account of this period is found in E. Herman Hespelt, "Fernán Caballero, A Study of Her Life and Works" (Unpublished Dissertation), Ithaca: Cornell University, 1925.

Chapter Two

1. José F. Montesinos, *Introducción a una historia de la novela en España, en el siglo XIX* (Madrid: Editorial Castalia, 1966); Reginald F. Brown, *La novela española, 1700-1850* (Madrid: Servicio de Publicaciones del Ministro de Educación Nacional, 1953); and E. Allison Peers, *A History of the Romantic Movement in Spain*, provide very ample bibliographies on the quantitative wealth of the Spanish novel before 1850.

2. Balzac is undoubtedly the author most quoted by Fernán Caballero within her works, as introductory sentences to chapters, and in the correspondence.

3. The problem of the style of *The Sea Gull* is complicated because of the lack of the original version in French, probably discarded by Mora, and the uncertainties about the alterations made by the translator, who was also an editor, and thus on his own about the insertion of ideas, words, etc.

4. This confirmation of the contemporary period as the setting marked a clear emphasis upon the Realistic qualities of *The Sea Gull*, and Ochoa, in calling attention to Fernán Caballero's resemblance to Scott, stressed the *Waverley* novels rather than the works set in the medieval or remote eras (V, 433-41).

5. Ochoa's objections to the adulterous love of Marisalada for Pepe Vera are difficult to understand in view of the vivid characterization and the obvious moral lessons derived from the affair by the author; but the critic is likewise on shaky ground in his paradoxical remarks that good dramas but not good novels are written by Spaniards (*Ibid.*).

6. Víctor Fuentes, "Sobre realismo y realidad social en las novelas de Fernán Caballero," *Duquesne Hispanic Review*, VII (1968), 20-21.

7. *Ibid.*, p. 14.

8. Herrero, *Fernán Caballero*, pp. 13-14.

9. "Fernán Caballero," *Poesia e non poesia* (Bari: Laterza, 1923), pp. 207-25.

10. *Ibid.*, p. 225.

11. Galdós ironically wrote this comment for the prologue to the first edition in 1882 of *El sabor de la tierruca* (*The Taste of the Big Earth*) by Pereda, not always an uncritical defender, but certainly a follower of Fernán Caballero's regionalism.

12. Pitollet, "Les premiers essais littéraires," IX, 288, quoting the letter of 1845 to Dr. Julius, perhaps the earliest indication of Fernán Caballero's formulation of her novelistic ideas.

13. Valencina, *Cartas de Fernán Caballero*, p. 39, quoting a letter of October 15, 1852.

14. This footnote is omitted in the B. A. E. edition of the *Obras*, but is found in the edition of the Colección de Escritores Castellanos, II, 288-89.

15. Herrero, *Fernán Caballero*, pp. 167-83, identifies in real life characters from the salon of the Countess of Algar in *The Sea Gull*.

16. Ochoa's reaction seems to be that the characters in these drawing room scenes had little basis in fact, or certainly did not add to the local color atmosphere (V, 438).

17. Montesinos, *Fernán Caballero*, p. 71.

18. *Ibid.*, p. 18.

19. José F. Montesinos, "Un esbozo de Fernán Caballero," *Volkstum und Kultur der Romanen*, III (1930), 239.

20. Castro Calvo, "estudio preliminar," p. cxiii; José F. Montesinos, "Notas sueltas sobre la fortuna de Balzac en España," *Revue de Littérature Comparée*, XXIV (1950), 309-38.

21. Croce, "Fernán Caballero," 207-25. Benito Brancaforte, "Benedetto Croce and the Theory of Popularism in Spanish Literature," *Hispanic Review*, XXXVIII (1970), 67-79, summarizes that "although Croce admits that the author in her naive missionary spirit uses and misuses art for any edifying purpose, and although her verbosity, the frequent interpolations of pious thoughts and the feeble structure of her novels are mentioned, nevertheless according to Croce she

belongs to the tradition of Cervantes and the author of *Lazarillo*" (p. 78).

22. Fuentes, "Sobre realismo y realidad social," p. 14, refers to Donoso Cortés as a major influence upon Fernán Caballero's philosophy and ideology, both writing at the same time, the former in the area of ideas and the latter as a novelist, with "the same vision of the world." A few scattered references in the letters but favorable comments in the works acknowledge the impact of Donoso Cortés, admitted also by Montesinos and Herrero.

Chapter Three

1. E. Herman Hespelt, "The Genesis of *La familia de Alvareda*," *Hispanic Review*, II (1934), 179-201; Montesinos, *Fernán Caballero*, pp. 143, 157-58.

2. Hespelt's edition of *La familia de Alvareda* (New York: Ginn, 1918) offers, especially in the introduction, interesting explanations for the popularity of this novel for English-speaking audiences as a work very representative of the Spanish spirit.

3. Ernest Jareño, edición, introducción y notas, *La familia de Alvareda* (Madrid: Anaya, 1971), pp. 22-31; Montesinos, *Fernán Caballero*, pp. 167, 169-78.

4. The scholarly importance of *The Family of Alvareda* for these critics, and the attendant regret, is that Realism appeared very early in Spain and that Fernán Caballero missed the opportunity to rank among the leading Europeans, such as Balzac and Dickens.

5. José F. Montesinos, *Costumbrismo y novela. Ensayo sobre el redescubrimiento de la realidad española* (Madrid: Castalia, 1965), 2nd edition, finds a reason for Fernán Caballero's success, as well as the triumph of the Realists, in "that humble world of things" (p. 8).

6. Antoine de Latour, "Fernán Caballero," *Le Correspondant*, August 25, 1857, p. 620, indicated that *The Family of Alvareda* rather than *The Sea Gull* was the first major novel of Fernán Caballero; but the researches of E. Herman Hespelt and Stanley T. Williams about her friendship with Washington Irving led securely to the recognition of the earlier work.

7. Curiously, Fernán Caballero, in her remarks on *Don Quijote*, shows no overwhelming admiration for this masterpiece; and she objects to the structure at times of the Cervantine novel.

8. E. Herman Hespelt and Stanley T. Williams, "Washington Irving's Notes to Fernán Caballero's Stories," *Publications of the Modern Language Association*, XXIX (1934), 1130-32.

9. Montesinos, *Fernán Caballero*, p. 54.

10. Jareño, *La familia de Alvareda*, p. 22.

11. Another example of the lack of an authoritative edition of

Fernán Caballero's works is the absence of this prologue from the B. A. E. edition of Calvo Castro and that of the Colección de Escritores Castellanos. The text used here is found in the new edition by Mellado (Madrid, 1861), pp. vi-vii.

12. *Ibid.*, p. vii.

13. "I do not claim to write *novels,* but local color sketches, portraits, accompanied by reflections and descriptions . . ." (Valencina, *Cartas,* p. 39); "I have repeated several times that I do not write novels, since the tendency of my little works is to combat the novelistic, a subtle venom in the good and plain path of real life" (*La Ilustración,* V [1853], 33-34).

14. Hespelt, "The Genesis," pp. 193-94; Hespelt and Williams, "Washington Irving's Notes," p. 1130.

15. Montesinos, *Fernán Caballero,* p. 104.

16. Their conclusions are founded, in addition to critical analyses, on the studies of Hespelt and Williams, already indicated, and also on the following articles: Hespelt and Williams, "Two Unpublished Anecdotes by Fernán Caballero Preserved by Washington Irving," *Modern Language Notes,* XLIX (1934), 25-31; Hespelt, "The Portorican Episode in the Life of Fernán Caballero," *Revista de Estudios Hispánicos,* I (1928), 162-67.

17. Asensio, "Fernán Caballero y la novela contemporánea," pp. 71-72; Coloma, *Recuerdos,* pp. 120-23, invents some dialogue and tries to show Fernán Caballero's emotional reaction about the village account.

18. The source of the somewhat garbled version is mentioned in the various renditions by Williams, "Washington Irving and Fernán Caballero," p. 361.

19. Hespelt and Williams, "Washington Irving's Notes," pp. 1131-32.

20. *Ibid.*, p. 1132.

21. *Ibid.*

22. Hespelt, "The Genesis," p. 183.

23. Williams, "Washington Irving and Fernán Caballero," p. 362.

24. Hespelt, "The Genesis," p. 183.

25. Heinermann, *Cecilia Böhl de Faber,* depicts conclusively her anxieties and reactions during 1849; and she writes to Hartzenbusch: "Before ending this, I am going to ask you a favor—if you have the spare time: read the *familia Alvareda* which came out in the Heraldo September of last year—it is a painting of the people, as I believe, that only I can make so *graphic,* because of the fact that I have lived in the country and I have studied it," Letter of February 15, 1850, pp. 113-14.

26. Hespelt, "The Genesis," pp. 194-95; 199-200.

27. *Ibid.*, pp. 188-89.
28. *Ibid.*, p. 189.
29. *Ibid.*, p. 194.
30. *Ibid.*, p. 200.
31. *Ibid.*, p. 201; Montesinos, *Fernán Caballero*, praises *The Family of Alvareda* as "her first great novel . . . an austere tale, detailed . . . the tragic sense of Andalusian life . . . ," pp. 54-55.

Chapter Four

1. Hespelt, "The Portorican Episode," pp. 162-67; Herrero, *Fernán Caballero*, pp. 200-217.
2. Herrero, *Fernán Caballero*, p. 336.
3. Heinermann, *Cecilia Böhl de Faber*, pp. 119-51, provides in letters 12-27 proof of the concern of Fernán Caballero about *Clemencia*.
4. Herrero evidently finds in *Clemencia* the key to much of Fernán Caballero's life and her art in general, with his thesis centered around the evolution of this novel as an outstanding creative endeavor.
5. Chapters eight and nine, pp. 36-45, comprise the brief description of the heroine's first marriage (*Obras*, II).
6. The most glaring and inexcusable defect of the Castro Calvo edition of the *Obras* is the omission of the third part of *Clemencia* with no indication to the unwary reader that the novel has not ended with the second part. The third part of *Clemencia* used here is located in the Colección de Escritores Castellanos, III, 361-538; and this particular passage is on p. 468.
7. *Clemencia*, Colección de Escritores Castellanos, III, 400.
8. *Ibid.*, 400-404. Balzac serves as the principal support for Clemencia in this discussion as well as in the debates with Sir George Percy, and the French novelist perhaps plays a greater role in this novel than in any other work of Fernán Caballero.
9. There are also minor but recurrent antipathies expressed throughout the works against bullfighting.
10. Her sensitivity about the implications of *Lágrimas* is seen in these letters: Colección de Escritores Castellanos, XIV (1912), *passim*.
11. Fuentes, "Sobre realismo y realidad social," p. 21.
12. *Ibid.*, p. 18.
13. José F. Montesinos, *Elia* (Madrid: Alianza Editorial, 1968), prólogo, pp. 7-25; Javier Herrero, "El 'Schlosser' de Fernán Caballero," *Romanische Forschungen*, LXXIV (1962), 404-12.
14. Another important element of *Elia* is that the novel was composed early in Fernán Caballero's career, an indication of her

awareness about the tragic circumstances of Spanish politics (Pitollet, "Les premiers essais littéraires," IX, 288).

15. Some indication of the political complications aroused by this novel, in particular, is observed in Fernán Caballero's later title of *Tres almas de Dios* (*Three Souls of God*) as less provocative than the more effective designation of *Un servilón y un liberalito* (*A Loyalist and a Liberal*).

16. There stands out in various novels and stories an evident symbolism in the names of characters, usually bestowed upon the less appealing actors in the works.

17. Montesinos, *Fernán Caballero*, pp. 71-85.

18. Valencina, *Cartas de Fernán Caballero*; *Epistolario* of the Collección de Escritores Castellanos; Alberto López Argüello, *Epistolario de Fernán Caballero* (Barcelona: Sucesores de Juan Gili, 1922). These collections of letters, after 1853 for the most part, supply the constant self-doubts of Fernán Caballero about her accomplishments.

19. Montesinos, *Fernán Caballero*, p. 71.

20. Calvo Castro's apparent purpose is to arrange the works in order of importance first, and secondly in some chronological manner.

21. Montesinos, *Fernán Caballero*, p. 91, explains as part of his arguments about Fernán Caballero's writings that the digressive, sermonizing aspects were the defects of her Romantic education.

22. Castro Calvo, "estudio preliminar," p. clvi, is especially convinced of the resemblances, in addition to the use of letters as the device in both books.

23. *Ibid.*, p. clxviii.

24. The tepid reaction of critics, and apparently readers, to the work, together with Fernán Caballero's lack of preoccupations about the novel may be the further evidence that the public mood was an uppermost consideration behind her literary contributions.

25. This mention of Longfellow antedates previous knowledge, seemingly, of the American poet's reception in Spain: John De Lancey Ferguson, *American Literature in Spain* (New York: Columbia University Press, 1916), p. 109.

26. Her own uncertainty about the designation of *La farisea* is seen in these letters: "A social study or contemporary local color sketch has appeared . . ." (*Epistolario* of the Colección de Escritores Castellanos, p. 391) and "It cannot be called a novel or even a *relación*; it is the painting of two characters" (*Ibid.*, p. 405).

Chapter Five

1. The correspondence, in fact, reveals an increasingly evident annoyance at the perplexed critics who were attempting to classify her books during the years of greatest popularity, and especially after

her literary decline, so that there is a repetitious pattern about these worries in all the major unpublished letters (Heinermann, Argüello, *Epistolario*, Valencina).

2. Fernán Caballero quotes from the "Histoires extraordinaires" of Poe (V, 307) and, curiously, her story, "Dicha y suerte," was included in Poe's first publication in Spain, a volume of the *Historias extraordinarias* in 1858 (Ferguson, *American Literature in Spain,* p. 229).

3. Knowledge of the Bécquer family in Sevilla seems evident by Fernán Caballero, a fellow Sevillian: she refers to the poet's uncle, Joaquín, with whom Gustavo Adolfo studied painting; and she also reacts very defensively on occasion but in passing to a Sevillian's articles about her writings in *El Contemporáneo* (*The Contemporary*), with the possibility that the critic might have been Gustavo Adolfo, who was collaborating actively on the newspaper.

4. Andrés Soria, *Cuentos andaluces* (Madrid: Alcalá, 1966), estudio y edición, pp. 30-31.

5. José F. Montesinos, "Un esbozo de Fernán Caballero," *Volkstum und Kultur der Romanen,* III (1930), 232-57, using a manuscript found in Vienna, has analyzed with his usual care this character study or "physiology."

6. *Ibid.*; cf. also Pitollet, "Les premiers essais littéraires," about the development of this sketch.

7. Castro Calvo, "estudio preliminar," p. clxv.

8. *Ibid.*, pp. cxlviii-cxlix; Montesinos, *Fernán Caballero,* p. 148, lists the bibliographical references about this story—a clear example about the writing, translation, magazine publication, editorial queries, and concern regarding reactions to the work.

9. Aurelio M. Espinosa, *Cuentos populares españoles* (Madrid: C. S. I. C., 1946), 3 vols.; Mariano Baquero Goyanes, *El cuento español en el siglo XIX* (Madrid: Aguirre, 1949); relate critically and with chronological bibliographies the contributions of Fernán Caballero to the short story.

10. V, 65; Charles de Mazade, "Le roman de moeurs en Espagne. Fernán Caballero et ses récits," *Revue des Deux Mondes,* November 25, 1858, pp. 352-80.

11. Montesinos, *Elia,* p. 25.

Chapter Six

1. Montesinos stresses that Fernán Caballero's fame swung sharply, and unjustly, from the excessive praise of Ochoa to the harsh attacks after 1870 (*Fernán Caballero,* pp. 105-39). Montesinos has consistently in his several invaluable studies called attention to the important role of Fernán Caballero, historically and as a pathfinder.

2. An informative, incisive treatment of Fernán Caballero's fellow woman novelist of the nineteenth century is provided by Walter T. Pattison, *Emilia Pardo Bazán* (New York: Twayne, 1971).

3. Menéndez Pelayo, at that time, was considered perhaps as a severe critic of Fernán Caballero; but his opinions, expressed in various writings, were not sufficiently collated for a balanced judgment. Also, the adverse—and astute—recognition of Fernán Caballero's defects was probably welcomed by her ideological and literary opponents. Cf. *Obras completas,* ed. Bonilla y San Martín, Madrid, 1911-1913, 21 vols.; or "Edicíon nacional," directed by M. Artigas and E. Sánchez Reyes, Madrid, 1940-1957, 65 vols., for the problem of determining within Menéndez Pelayo's prodigious output his unified approach to Fernán Caballero.

4. The analyses by Montesinos, especially, and also Herrero, about Fernán Caballero's popularity in the nineteenth century outside Spain can be followed by a glance at the several worthwhile school and popular editions, supervised, for example, by Hespelt and Montesinos, respectively, with enlightening introductions. In view of the unsatisfactory state of the editions of Fernán Caballero's works, these well-prepared books by recognized scholars have a rewarding place in any bibliographical lists. Four theses on Fernán Caballero apparently represent the extent of interest among graduate degrees (Cf. James R. Chatham & Enrique Ruiz-Fornells, *Dissertations in Hispanic Languages and Literatures. An Index of Dissertations Completed in the United States and Canada, 1876-1966* (Lexington: The University Press of Kentucky, 1970), pp. 54-55.

Selected Bibliography

The absence of a reliable edition of Fernán Caballero's works, deplored by Montesinos and Herrero as well as other researchers, has required the use of different texts in this book in the attempt to provide an accurate source for references. This unhappy compromise has resulted in the use of the B. A. E. edition with the substitution of the Colección de Escritores Castellanos when necessary. A suggestion for readers of Fernán Caballero (accepting the methods of Montesinos and Herrero, likewise) would be to follow that admittedly tortuous path, keeping in mind the other editions and also the individual texts of the works, still appearing principally in this country and Spain.

This selected bibliography is presented only as a starting point and is not necessarily intended as a definitive list of references. Items consulted and deemed useful for this study, and the sources (whether important or perhaps of limited value) listed most often about Fernán Caballero are the criteria for inclusion in the following pages. The correspondence has been listed as a primary source, of course, but the commentaries by the editors are also classified and discussed under the individual publications of letters.

PRIMARY SOURCES

1. Editions

Obras completas. The *Obras completas* have appeared in six different editions, all in Madrid. The first two were by Mellado in 1855-1858 (19 vols.) and the Nueva Edición of 1861-1864 (16 vols.). An edition of 14 volumes was published by Sáenz de Jubera in 1865-1893, and a 17-volume edition was made in 1902-1907 by Antonio de Romero e Hijos de Guijarro. In the Colección de Escritores Castellanos 17 volumes were published in 1905-1914. Rubiños issued a 17-volume edition in 1917-1921.

Obras de Fernán Caballero (Madrid: Biblioteca de Autores Españoles, 1961), vols. CXXXVI-CXL.

2. Correspondence

Epistolario (Madrid: Hernando, 1912), Vol. 14 of the *Obras completas* of the Colección de Escritores Castellanos. A collection of 159

letters (including two poems dedicated to Fernán Caballero),
written after 1853; important for her reactions to the works
during and after publication.

HEINERMANN, THEODOR. *Cecilia Böhl de Faber (Fernán Caballero)
y Juan Eugenio Hartzenbusch. Una correspondencia inédita*
(Madrid: Espasa-Calpe, 1944). Probably the most significant
set of letters, fifty-nine, written to her influential friend, from
1849 until 1869, which reveal explanations and motives for the
novels, in particular; the introductions and analyses of the individual letters offer an excellent work of scholarship, which
changed many existing ideas about Fernán Caballero, especially
those of Coloma.

LOPEZ ARGÜELLO, ALBERTO. *Epistolario de Fernán Caballero. Una
colección de cartas inéditas de la novelista* (Barcelona: Sucesores
de Juan Gili, 1922). Eighty letters, beginning in 1855, and noteworthy principally because of the recipients, who were, in
general, critics, and with whom Fernán Caballero could discuss
more frankly her literary views.

MONTOTO, SANTIAGO. *Cartas inéditas de Fernán Caballero* (Madrid:
S. Aguirre Torre, 1961). These letters are especially revealing
of more personal details of Fernán Caballero's life, e.g., the near
affair in England with "Federico Cuthbert"; the importance
resides in the new relationships established between the books,
such as *Clemencia*, and the author's biography.

MOREL-FATIO, ALFRED. "Fernán Caballero d'après sa correspondance
avec Antoine de Latour," *Bulletin Hispanique*, III (1901), 152-
294. Fragments of the extensive correspondence with Latour,
with the purpose of reaching some generalizations and conclusions about the complete letters; the selections are aimed
at an artistic rather than a biographical interest in Fernán
Caballero.

VALENCINA, DIEGO DE. *Cartas de Fernán Caballero* (Madrid: Sucesores
de Hernando, 1919). A very extensive collection of letters to
many correspondents; the fragmentary nature of the material,
although essential for any research, suggests that the priest-
editor omitted items to which he may have personally objected.

SECONDARY SOURCES

1. Books

COLOMA, LUIS. *Recuerdos de Fernán Caballero* (Madrid: Editorial
"Razón y Fe," 1949), XVII. A charming, romantic account of
Fernán Caballero's life and works, which has enjoyed an un-
deserved reputation as authoritative for too many years. Publi-

cation of Heinermann's book on Fernán Caballero's correspondence with Hartzenbusch and subsequent contributions of Montoto and Montesinos, in particular, have reduced Coloma's "remembrances" to very low value.

HERRERO, JAVIER. *Fernán Caballero: un nuevo planteamiento* (Madrid: Editorial Gredos, 1963). Sound critical scholarship with emphasis on Fernán Caballero's parental background and the biographical facets of her career as the key to her work, certain books, in particular, such as *Clemencia*.

MONTESINOS, JOSÉ F. *Fernán Caballero. Ensayo de justificación* (México: El Colegio de México, 1961). An incisive, excellent investigation of Fernán Caballero's importance, assets, and liabilities; the Andalusian backgrounds, the narrative observations, and the constant Romanticism stand out clearly; the sermonizing and the moralizing detract from her stature; and the recognition is needed of her revolutionary development of the modern novel.

PALMA, ANGÉLICA. *Fernán Caballero, la novelista novelable* (Madrid: Espasa-Calpe, 1931). A popular biography, with little reliance on scholarship except for Coloma's *recuerdos*, and an effort to look for the melodramatic aspects of Fernán Caballero's life.

ROMANO, JULIO. *Fernán Caballero (La alondra y la tormenta)*, (Madrid: Editora Nacional, 1949). A completely inadequate rendition of the biographical facts, with imaginary dialogues, and no attempt to discuss the works seriously.

2. Articles

ASENSIO, JOSÉ MARÍA. "Fernán Caballero y la novela contemporánea," prologue to Vol. I of the *Obras completas* (Madrid: Colección de Escritores Castellanos, 1893). An accurate, critical endeavor at the biographical record of Fernán Caballero; a detailed analysis of her contributions to the Spanish novel, often overlooked by popularizers, and still useful for valid insights.

CASTRO CALVO, JOSÉ MARÍA. "Estudio preliminar," *Obras de Fernán Caballero* (Madrid: Biblioteca de Autores Españoles, 1961), I, vii-clxxxvii. The defects of this particular edition are seen in this introduction: careless proofreading, inadequate bibliographical references, lack of editorial care (the bibliography is not even arranged alphabetically). Judgments are frequently based on impressionistic interpretations, but the overall view is useful as a starting point for some understanding of the woman and the work.

BRANCAFORTE, BENITO. "Benedetto Croce and the Theory of Popularism in Spanish Literature," *Hispanic Review*, XXXVIII (1970),

69-79. Summarizes the Italian critic's theories on the popular spirit as the central theme of a great literature, endeavors to analyze the high praise for Fernán Caballero, and provides a more objective criticism of the latter's role in Spanish literature.

CROCE, BENEDETTO. "Fernán Caballero," *Poesia e non poesia* (Bari: Laterza, 1923), 207-25. An important statement by a major critic on the neglected reputation of Fernán Caballero; an exaggerated claim to her status as the most significant Spanish writer of the nineteenth century because of her convenient place within the theory of popularism.

GABRIEL Y RUIZ DE APODACA, FERNANDO DE. *Estar de más, relación, y Magdalena, obra inédita, precedidas de una noticia biográfica* (Sevilla: Gironés y Orduña, 1878). The first accurate, and still dependable, source for the main outlines of Fernán Caballero's life; later studies have amplified and clarified this generally neglected material.

HEINERMANN, THEODOR. "Dichtung und Wahrheit über die Gaviota Fernán Caballeros," *Romanische Forschungen*, LVI (1942), 313-24. The definitive explanation of the background about the publication of *The Sea Gull* with the resulting loss of confidence in Coloma's version and the romantic legend about Fernán Caballero's sudden appearance as a writer in 1849.

HERRERO, JAVIER. "El 'Schlosser' de Fernán Caballero," *Romanische Forschungen*, LXXIV (1962), 404-12. The earlier sketch of Herrero's theses in *Fernán Caballero*; an introductory, well-organized achievement in understanding the personal, psychological aspects behind the literary activities.

HESPELT, E. HERMAN. "A Second Pseudonym of Cecilia Böhl de Arrom," *Modern Language Notes*, XLI (1926), 123-25. A brief yet revealing indication of Fernán Caballero's attempt at anonymity by her use in 1850 of the name "León de Lara" for the story, *Callar en vida y perdonar en muerte*.

————. "The Portorican Episode in the Life of Fernán Caballero," *Revista de Estudios Hispánicos*, I (1928), 162-67. The short, tragic residence in Puerto Rico as the unhappy wife and widow of her first husband left memories and scars that appeared later in Fernán Caballero's works.

————. "The Genesis of 'La Familia de Alvareda,'" *Hispanic Review*, II (1934), 179-201. A decisive investigation into the various stages of the composition of *The Family of Alvareda*, proving the importance of this novel as Fernán Caballero's first and very early excursion into the field of literature and Realism.

HESPELT, E. HERMAN and STANLEY T. WILLIAMS. "Two Unpublished Anecdotes by Fernán Caballero Preserved by Washington Irving," *Modern Language Notes*, XLIX (1934), 25-31. Impressive evidence about Washington Irving's knowledge of Fernán Caballero's writings and the latter's extensive, dedicated collection of anecdotes and stories intended for future use.

—————. "Washington Irving's Notes to Fernán Caballero's Stories," *Publications of the Modern Language Association*, XXIX (1934), 1129-39. More confirmation of the American writer's knowledge of Fernán Caballero's wealth of local color material and folklore, especially the outline of major stories, such as *The Family of Alvareda* and *Elia*.

HORRENT, J. "Sur *La Gaviota* de Fernán Caballero," *Revue des Langues Vivantes*, XXXII (1966), 227-37. The importance of this Realistic novel is emphasized on aesthetic terms in addition to the recognized role in literary histories.

LATOUR, ANTOINE DE. "Littérature Espagnole. Fernán Caballero," *Le Correspondant*, August 25, 1857, pp. 605-34. An influential, lengthy analysis of Fernán Caballero's importance in European literature in foreign periodicals, written by a friend, but objective and still valuable for the early recognition of ideas, themes, etc., in her writings.

MAZADE, CHARLES DE. "Le roman de moeurs en Espagne. Fernán Caballero et ses récits," *Revue des Deux Mondes*, November 25, 1858, pp. 352-80. Another European, significantly French, report in which Fernán Caballero enjoyed a very sympathetic reception: the serious changes she effected in the Spanish novel by the use of local color and indigenous elements.

MONTESINOS, JOSÉ F. "Un esbozo de Fernán Caballero," *Volkstum und Kultur der Romanen*, III (1930), 232-57. The foreshadowing of the Spanish critic's broader interests in the work of Fernán Caballero, together with attention called to her merits at a time of low scholarly interest.

OCHOA, EUGENIO DE. "Juicio crítico de *La Gaviota*," *La España*, August 25, 1849 (Reprinted in the B.A.E. edition, CXL, 433-41.). Still the justifiable starting point, historically and aesthetically, for all serious review of the criticism of Fernán Caballero's work, especially *The Sea Gull*. Some arguments, however, such as the theory of the Spanish novel, seem out of place, although recognition of foreign models is impressive and accurate.

PITOLLET, CAMILLE. "Les premiers essais littéraires de Fernán Caballero," *Bulletin Hispanique*, IX (1907), 67-86, 286-302; X (1908), 286-305, 378-96. An outstanding contribution to scholarship with much supporting evidence about the early, important development of Fernán Caballero's interest and attainments in literature; the focal point for investigation of her career before the appearance of *The Sea Gull.*

——————. "A propos de Fernán Caballero et de M. Montesinos," *Bulletin Hispanique,* XXXIII (1931), 335-40. A moderating voice about the laudatory analysis of Montesinos regarding Fernán Caballero, with the recognition that more research seems needed for a truer evaluation.

——————. "Deux mots encore sur Fernán Caballero," *Bulletin Hispanique,* XXXIV (1932), 153-60. A sharp critique of Angélica Palma's book on Fernán Caballero, with the lack of a solid biography as the cause for much misrepresentation; interesting for the points raised for any future reliable effort in this direction.

WILLIAMS, STANLEY T. "Washington Irving and Fernán Caballero," *Journal of English and Germanic Philology,* XXIX (1930), 352-66. A subtle and well-based approach to the mutual collaboration and influence of the two writers during their acquaintanceship, with attention called to Fernán Caballero's possible influence in Irving's Spanish interests and works.

WOLF, FERDINAND. "Über den realistischen Roman Spaniens," *Jahrbuch für romanische und englische Literatur,* I (1859), 247-97. A relevant, organized survey of the arrival and growth of the Realistic novel in Spain, giving much attention to Fernán Caballero's contribution, and urging her acknowledgment as a major European novelist; an influential article by an important critic.

Index